Benjamin Franklin, Swimmer

An Illustrated History

Benjamin Franklin, Swimmer

An Illustrated History

Sarah B. Pomeroy

American Philosophical Society Press
Philadelphia

Transactions of the
American Philosophical Society
Held at Philadelphia
For Promoting Useful Knowledge
Volume 110, Part 1

U.S. ISSN: 0065-9746

978-1-60618-101-0 (print)

978-1-60618-106-5 (ebook)

The publisher has no responsibility for the persistence or accuracy of URLs for external or third-party Internet websites referred to in this publication and does not guarantee that any content on such websites is, or will remain, acccurate or appropriate.

Library of Congress Cataloging-in-Publication Data

Names: Pomeroy, Sarah B., author.
Title: Benjamin Franklin, swimmer : an illustrated history / Sarah B. Pomeroy.
Description: Philadelphia : American Philosophical Society Press, 2021. | Series: Transactions of the American Philosophical Society, 0065-9746 ; 110 | Includes bibliographical references and index. | Text in English, with some text in French. | Summary: "This is the first book that focuses on Benjamin Franklin as a swimmer. Franklin thought swimming a valuable activity and swam whenever he could wherever he was. We can see Franklin's personality emerge through the lens of swimming, which offered him entrée into London society as a young man. The book includes excerpts from the journal of Benjamin Franklin Bache, Franklin's grandson"--Provided by publisher.
Identifiers: LCCN 2021010644 (print) | LCCN 2021010645 (ebook) | ISBN 9781606181010 (paperback) | ISBN 9781606181065 (kindle edition)
Subjects: LCSH: Franklin, Benjamin, 1706-1790. | Swimmers--United States--Biography. | Bache, Benjamin Franklin, 1801-1881Family. | Swimming--History--18th century.
Classification: LCC GV838.F68 P66 2021 (print) | LCC GV838.F68 P66 2021 (ebook) | DDC 797.21--dc23
LC record available at https://lccn.loc.gov/2021010644
LC ebook record available at https://lccn.loc.gov/2021010645

Cover design by Eugenia B. González based on a black-and-white woodcut by Everard Digby (see Figure 1.5).

To Jordana and Jeremy
and to the memory of Ali

Contents

Chronology for Benjamin Franklin, Swimmer *ix*
Abbreviations xi
Author's Note xiii
Introduction xv

1 A Lifetime of Swimming 1

2 Why Swim? 19

3 Swimming in France 33

Epilogue: Water, Water, Everywhere 55

Appendix: French Text of Jacques Barbeu-Dubourg's Letter to Franklin 69

Acknowledgments 79

Index 83

Chronology
for *Benjamin Franklin, Swimmer*

1706 Benjamin Franklin born in Boston
1723 to Philadelphia
1724 to London
1726 to Philadelphia
1757 to London
1762 to Philadelphia
1767 to France
1769 Second voyage to France
1769 Benjamin Franklin Bache (Benny) born
1771 Franklin begins the *Autobiography*
1775 to Philadelphia
1776 to France with Temple and Benny
1785 to Philadelphia
1790 Benjamin Franklin dies
1798 Benjamin Franklin Bache dies

Abbreviations

The following abbreviations appear in this book:

Autobiography = The Autobiography of Benjamin Franklin

The authoritative version is Labaree, Leonard W., Ketcham, Ralph L., Boatfield, Helen C., and Finerman, Helene H., eds. 1964. *The Autobiography of Benjamin Franklin* (2nd edition). New Haven, CT: Yale University Press. With Foreword by Edmund S. Morgan. Unless otherwise noted, references to the *Autobiography* in this book are to this edition.

The *Autobiography* is also available in many other versions. For example, the version available at http://www.gutenberg.org/files/20203/20203-h/20203-h.htm modernizes Franklin's spelling.

Chaplin, Joyce E., ed. 2012. *Benjamin Franklin's Autobiography*. New York: W. W. Norton. This volume retains the eighteenth-century spelling and punctuation.

Excerpts from the *Autobiography* are also available in *The Papers of Benjamin Franklin*, Vol. 1.

PBF = The Papers of Benjamin Franklin.

Labaree, Leonard W., et al., eds. 1959–. *The Papers of Benjamin Franklin* (43 vols. to date). New Haven, CT: Yale University Press.

Thévenot = Thévenot, Melchisédec. 1972. *The Art of Swimming* (reprint of Third London Edition). Paris, 1696; trans. London, 1699; third edition, London, 1789, New York, 1972).

Author's Note

////////////////////////

Why am I—a historian of Greece and Rome—interested in Benjamin Franklin? I became a member of the American Philosophical Society in 2014. I was elected because of my pioneering scholarly work in the history of women in antiquity. Members meet twice a year in Franklin's corner of Philadelphia. At our meetings we always see his benevolent portrait hanging behind the speaker's podium.

Then Dr. Márcia Balisciano, Director of Benjamin Franklin House, London, invited me to be the first Lady Joan Reid Author in Residence for Children's Literature at Franklin House. Franklin House is the only dwelling where Benjamin Franklin lived that is still extant.

In writing a book about Benjamin Franklin, I felt it appropriate to adhere to his advice, offered in "On Literary Style, 2 August 1733," in *The Pennsylvania Gazette*: "I have thought in general, that whoever would write so as not to displease good Judges, should have particular Regard to these three Things, viz. That his Performance be *smooth, clear,* and *short.*"[1]

Because I am a historian, I have arranged the chapters chronologically. Furthermore, as in my other historical writings, I use material and artistic evidence as primary sources with the same valence as written texts. In this book, paintings illustrate long-lost landscapes and bodies of water where Franklin swam. Several images come from books on swimming that Franklin read. This attention to visual sources is new in Franklin historical studies.

In this book direct quotations from Benjamin Franklin and from Benjamin Franklin Bache are printed in italics.

---

[1] *PBF*, vol. 1 (1959), 328–331. *Pennsylvania Gazette*, August 2, 1733; also draft: Historical Society of Pennsylvania = Sparks, vol. 2 (1836), 553.

"He" is generally used to refer to a swimmer because in Franklin's writings only men and boys swim.

Finally, I was drawn to this subject because I, too, am a swimmer.

Note on Images

This book was completed while the COVID-19 pandemic was raging. The museums, libraries, and other institutions that are the sources of most of the images were closed. The images that appear in this book are the best quality obtainable under such dire circumstances.

Sarah B. Pomeroy
Sag Harbor, New York

Introduction

B enjamin Franklin's earliest unique memories and first inventions are connected to swimming. In his *Autobiography*, after a traditional opening reviewing his family's history, his formal education, and his brief apprenticeship as a candlemaker, he wrote a long paragraph about his interest in the sea and in boats and swimming. Franklin's youthful inventions included swimming paddles and a method of kitesurfing; he boasted of these later in life. Yet this aspect of Franklin's biography has never been studied.

There are countless publications about Benjamin Franklin: some of which mention his swimming briefly in passing. This book is the first study that focuses on Franklin as a swimmer. The modern reader, especially the sedentary scholar, may be surprised at my choice of subject, considering this American icon's swimming of little importance when compared to his scientific discoveries and civic and political achievements. Franklin himself, however, thought swimming was of great value. He swam wherever and whenever he could, from boyhood through old age, and he chose to live close to rivers where swimming was possible.

Franklin's personality emerges through the lens of swimming. We see him clearly as a leader, an inventor, and a strong, proud man. As he was in many fields, he was self-taught. He interacted with family, friends, and acquaintances through swimming. As a young man in London, swimming offered him an entrée into British society. It is possible to trace Franklin's travels by noticing the places where he swam.

Franklin discusses swimming in his Letters and in his *Autobiography*. Friends and family also comment on his swimming. Though the evidence is sparse, varied references to swimming occur throughout Franklin's lifetime and in a variety of contexts. He praises swimming because it promotes health, hygiene, and safety—especially when people find themselves suddenly in the water. Therefore knowing how to swim was essential not only for a professional sailor but also for anyone who traveled by boat. In those days, travel by boat was common. In his *Autobiography* Franklin mentions taking boats and ferries on his first journey from Boston to Philadelphia and of course on his subsequent journeys: he records the perils and pleasures of these voyages in detail. Drowning was such a common occurrence that only disasters involving multiple deaths that destroyed entire families or boatloads attracted much attention.

The water played a decisive role in Franklin's life. Fearing ocean travel, Franklin's wife, Deborah, refused to join him in Europe. As a result they spent most of their married life apart.

When Franklin's grandson Benjamin Franklin Bache was in his care in France, Franklin allowed him to swim across the Seine, an activity that was fraught with danger from strong winds and passing ships. Benny's Journal[1] constitutes another important primary source for this book. The escapades in France of this engaging, literate teenager with a benevolent, indulgent chaperone have never before been published. Benny is an astute and likeable guide to the eighteenth century. There is no doubt that the Journal of Ben Franklin's grandson will be of great interest both to sophisticated younger readers and to scholars and students of Ben Franklin.

---

[1] See Chapter 3 for more information.

Chapter 1

A Lifetime of Swimming

Benjamin Franklin taught himself to swim when he was a boy. Swimming is just one of the many skills Ben taught himself. His parents were too poor to send him to school past the age of ten, so he became his own teacher. Ben was a natural swimmer who enjoyed swimming and never lost his enthusiasm for it. Later in life, when he persuaded others to learn to swim, he emphasized how easy it was; like much else, swimming was easy for him.

When Franklin was born on January 17, 1706, his family lived at 17 Milk Street in north Boston. When he was six they moved to the southwest corner of Hanover and Union Streets. Boston was virtually surrounded by water, with marshland (now known as "the Fens") in its interior. Ben's new home was just a short walk from the Mill Pond (Figure 1.1).[1] His father was a candlemaker and his mother helped out in the business. As the youngest son in a working-class family that eventually had 17 children, Ben was unsupervised and could spend much of his day in the water. He showed his skills as an inventor and leader at an early age when he organized his companions to carry out a complicated, mischievous deed to facilitate their fishing regardless of the tide:

> There was a Salt Marsh that bounded part of the Mill Pond, on the Edge of which at Highwater, we us'd to stand to fish for Minews. By much Trampling, we had made it a mere Quagmire. My Proposal was to build a Wharf there fit for us to stand upon, and I show'd my Comrades a large Heap of Stones which were intended for a new House near the Marsh, and which would very well suit our Purpose.

Working like an army of ants building an anthill, the boys constructed a wharf in a single evening. The theft was soon detected and punishment followed. Young Franklin drew a moral from the incident:

> Accordingly in the Evening when the Workmen were gone, I assembled a Number of my Playfellows, and working with them diligently like so many Emmets [ants], sometimes two or three to a Stone, we brought them all away and built our little Wharf. The next morning the Workmen were surpriz'd at Missing the Stones; which were found in our Wharf; Enquiry was made after the Removers; we were discovered and complain'd of; several of us were corrected by our Fathers; and tho' I pleaded the Usefulness of

---

[1] Massachusetts Historical Commission, "Boston's Mill Pond," 2014. http://www.sec.state.ma.us/mhc/mhcarchexhibitsonline/millpond.htm.

Figure 1.1 Part of a late seventeenth-century wharf at the Mill Pond.

––––––––––––––––––––

The Mill Pond was created from marshland during the middle of the seventeenth century. By means of dams, a channel, and floodgates, it was filled with saltwater from the harbor. As Franklin's description indicates, a salt marsh remained on the edge of the Mill Pond. Small boats could move through the pond and service the corn mills for which the pond was created. The pond needed to be dredged from time to time in order to prevent it from reverting to its natural state. Excavation finds from the pond include the late seventeenth-century wharf, a late eighteenth-century dock and bulkhead, and eighteenth-century houses.

Courtesy, Massachusetts Historical Commission, Office of the Secretary of the Commonwealth.

––––––––––––––––––––

the Work, mine convinc'd me that nothing was useful which was not honest.
(A 13–14)

There were no swimming pools in Colonial Boston (Figure 1.2). Pools were not constructed in America until the nineteenth century. In the eighteenth century, few lakes and rivers had been cleared of weeds and rushes or had their banks artificially fortified, and certainly not for the sake of recreational swimming. Swimmers might find themselves suddenly entangled: Treading water was not recommended if the water bottom was full of weeds and rushes. Early swimming manuals included advice on moving through the water when the legs were entangled or bound together

Figure 1.2 Boston in the eighteenth century. R. Byron, *View looking north and east from Fort Hill over the wharves* (ca. 1764).

"View of the watery North End of Boston in New England America and of Charles Town."

Photogravure. Boston Public Library, Print Department. Boston Pictorial Archive.[2]

(Figure 1.3). The swimmer was to flip the pair of legs in unison like a mermaid's tail.

Unlike most other sports, swimming does not require any equipment, not even special attire. Nevertheless Franklin designed two devices that could make swimming more efficient. His earliest memorable invention was a set of fins or paddles that he tried first on his feet (Figure 1.4). He discovered that they did not work well with the frog kick—the simultaneous sidewise movement of the legs to the bent position—which was the basic kick in those days. Then he put the paddles on his hands. The paddles improved his stroke, but he found that they made his wrists tired. Because he was swimming in a pond and later in rivers, not in a modern pool, he could not simply take the paddles off after using them awhile, but would have had to interrupt his swim to wade to the bank of the river and deposit the paddles. A commercial flexible material like rubber did not exist. His stiff wooden fins proved uncomfortable and difficult to use. Franklin's

---

[2] I am grateful to Gail J. Fithian for suggesting this image.

Figure 1.3 "To Swim having the Legs tied together."

"The Legs being bound either by Weeds, or otherwise, you must turn on your back, and lay your hands across on your breast, for in that posture you may gain the shore by striking your legs one against another, and holding them up as much as you can."

Melchisédec Thévenot, *The Art of Swimming* (Paris: 1696, translated London, 1699, henceforth cited as *Thévenot*), 44 and plate XXIV.

---

experiment with paddles showed that they began as a help but became a hindrance.

Many years after the fact Franklin proudly recalled:

When I was a boy, I made two oval palettes, each about ten inches long and six inches broad, with a hole for the thumb in order to retain it fast in the palm of my hand. They much resembled a painter's palette. In swimming, I pushed the edges of these forward and I struck the water with their flat surfaces as I drew them back. I remember I swam faster by means of these palettes, but they fatigued my wrists. I also fitted to the soles of my feet a kind of sandals, but I was not satisfied with them because I observed that the stroke is partly given by the inside of the feet and the ankles, and not entirely with the soles of the feet.[3]

---

[3] In a letter to Jacques Barbeu-Dubourg, March: Quillau l'aîne, Libraire, 1773. Translated extract of letter printed in Jacques Barbeu-Dubourg, ed., *Oeuvres de M. Franklin...* 2 vols. (Paris: Quillau l'aîne, Libraire, 1773), II, 258–61. Available at 626193 = 020-131a.html; see Chapter 3.

Figure 1.4 Twentieth-century fins and paddles.

The hand paddles and swim fins designed by Louis de Corlieu, Lieutenant Commander in the French Navy (1888–1967), are not so different from those created by Franklin.

Franklin is renowned for flying a kite during a thunderstorm in June 1752 to demonstrate the electrical force in lightning. Less well known is that, when he was young, he also tried using a kite for kitesurfing—a kind of parasurfing. Franklin's knowledge of navigation was the key to his success. The kite-surfer must lie on his back in the water while moving in the direction that enables him to gaze at the kite as he goes:

> When I was a boy, I amused myself one day with flying a paper kite, and
> approaching the bank of a pond which was near a mile broad, I tied the
> string to a stake, and the kite ascended to a very considerable height above

the pond while I was swimming. In a little time, being desirous of amusing myself with my kite and enjoying at the same time the pleasure of swimming, I returned; and, loosing from the stake the string with the little stick which was fastened to it, went again into the water where I found that, lying on my back and holding the stick in my hands, I was drawn along the surface of the water in a very agreeable manner. Having then engaged another boy to carry my clothes round the pond, to a place which I pointed out to him on the other side, I began to cross the pond with my kite, which carried me quite over without the least fatigue, and with the greatest pleasure imaginable. I was only obliged occasionally to halt a little in my course, and resist its progress, when it appeared that by following too quick, I lowered the kite too much; by doing which I occasionally made it rise again. (PBF, vol. 20, 133)

Some of the postures described in sixteenth- and seventeenth-century swimming manuals involved keeping the arms raised and were therefore useful for carrying clothing above the surface of the water (Figure 1.5). By swimming in this way, when the swimmer arrived at his destination, he could put on his dry clothes.

In America and Europe during the eighteenth century there were no proper bathing suits. Light-weight materials like Lycra had not been invented. In order not to be weighed down by wet clothing, men and boys swam naked (Figure 1.6), and women (being modest) did not swim at all, at least not in public. Though Franklin asserted that women were capable of being educated, he did not advocate teaching them how to swim. Later, when Franklin traveled to Europe, his wife, Deborah (1708–74; Figure 1.7), refused to accompany him, probably, at least in part, because she was afraid of ocean voyages because she did not know how to swim.

As part of his wholesome youthful agenda, when he was about 16 Franklin experimented with vegetarianism, even avoiding fish (A14, 36). He had read Plutarch, *On the Eating of Flesh.* Influenced by theories about the transmigration of the soul, Plutarch argues that eating meat is disgusting and unnatural, and that slaughtering innocent animals is a kind of murder. Franklin had also read Thomas Tryon's *The Way to Health, Long Life, and Happiness* (1697) and followed recipes in that book. When he was a teenager living independently, Franklin engaged a woman in his neighborhood to cook for him, using a list of forty vegetarian dishes (A 63). Along with a wide variety of vegetables, bread was central to the diet. Tryon included eggs and dairy, and allowed fish and "flesh fit to be eaten." Franklin annoyed his cook with his unusual requests. But he reports that when he ran away from Boston and was traveling to New York [in 1723], the crew caught some large cod. The smell of the fresh fish being cooked seduced

Figure 1.5 "Manum [sic] Erectio" (Swimming while carrying things above the water).

"When swimming with both arms up it is necessary to guard against constricting the chest."

Everard Digby, "Manum [sic] Erectio" in *De Arte Natandi* (London: Thomas Dawson, 1587), n.p.

Franklin into abandoning strict vegetarianism for a while. He justified eating fish because he observed that, when they were being

Figure 1.6 Thomas Eakins (1844–1916), *Swimming*, 1885.

About 100 years after Ben Franklin's lifetime, the Philadelphia artist Thomas Eakins in *Swimming* (also known as *The Swimming Hole* and *The Old Swimming Hole*) depicted men swimming at Dove Lake, an artificial lake in Mill Creek just outside Philadelphia.

Fort Worth, Texas: Amon Carter Museum of American Art. Goodrich catalog #190.

---

gutted, small fish were seen in their stomachs. He decided: "If you eat one another, I don't see why we mayn't eat you" (A 67–68). He advocated eating porridge at breakfast, referring to it as "Hot Water Gruel" (A 101). This warming dish was well suited to a person who was going to burn plenty of calories during the day. It consisted of cereal with toasted bread cubes and butter.[4] When he was young Ben Franklin drank less alcohol than most men of the time and therefore was later known as "the Water American" (A 99). It is interesting to note, however, that this sobriquet could also refer to his swimming and to his fascination with water.

In 1724 Franklin traveled to England to find work as a printer. As a young man in London, Franklin swam in the Thames (Figure 1.8). Though

---

[4] For the recipe, see Rae Katherine Eighmey, *Stirring the Pot with Benjamin Franklin* (Washington, DC: Smithsonian Books, 2018), 68.

Figure 1.7 Benjamin Wilson (1721–88) attributed, *Deborah Read Franklin*, 1758–59.
American Philosophical Society Museum.

this exercise was not common, he was not the first to do so. On June 5, 1711, Jonathan Swift wrote to a friend: "I am cruel thirsty this hot weather, I am just this minute going to swim."[5] The Thames was cleaner in the eighteenth century than it was later, but it was more shallow and wider

[5] Thomas Sheridan et al., eds., *Journal to Stella. The Works of the Rev. Jonathan Swift*, vol. 15, part 2, Letter xxiv, para. 5 (London: C. Bathurst, 1784).

Figure 1.8 William Marlow, *St. Paul's and Blackfriar's Bridge*, 1770–72.

Franklin's audience would have watched him from the boats, the shores of the Thames, and from the bridge.

Yale Center for British Art, Paul Mellon Collection, accession number B1976.7.54. Available at collections.britishart.yale.edu.

before the embankments were built. It was also tidal and currents could be treacherous. All kinds of ships plied the waters: Their captains would not have thought that they needed to be on the lookout for swimmers. Franklin was a powerful swimmer, but doubtless he had studied the river and chose auspicious conditions for his recreational swims and aquatic performances. He writes about one swimming adventure that occurred at a critical point in his life. He emphasizes his own bravery and bravado and glosses over the fact that his friends accompanied him and shielded him from the potential danger posed by passing ships.

In London, Franklin was a long-distance and exhibition swimmer. He also became a successful swimming instructor. In May or June 1726 he easily taught John Wygate (a friend who worked with him as a printer) and Wygate's friend how to swim in only two lessons: "at twice going into the River, and they soon became good Swimmers." The swimmers attracted a group of onlookers. Franklin responded to their interest by performing feats of swimming that required strength, endurance, and grace. As usual, he showed off: he even invented some new ways of performing in the water. He wrote that on this excursion he swam more than 3½ miles:

> *At the request of the company, whose Curiosity Wygate had excited, I stript and leapt in the River, and swam from near Chelsea to Blackfryars performing on the Way many Feats of Activity, both upon and under Water, that surpriz'd and pleas'd those to whom they were Novelties. -- I had from a Child been ever delighted with this Exercise, had studied and practis'd all Thévenot's Motions and Positions, added some of my own, aiming at graceful and easy as well as the Useful. All these I took this Occasion of exhibiting to the Company, and was much flatter'd by their Admiration.*
> (A 103–04)

The "feats of activity" Franklin mentions are various postures described and diagrammed in a swimming manual by Melchisédec Thévenot (A 104). Thévenot published *L'Art de Nager* in Paris in 1696. An English translation was published in London in 1699 as *The Art of Swimming*. In his *Autobiography* Franklin records that he had begun learning French in 1733; he therefore must have read the English version of Thévenot. The book included forty copperplate illustrations accompanied by verbal explanations of various positions that could be used in swimming; the diagrams were explicit enough that even a person who was barely literate could learn simply by looking at them. Although Thévenot does not credit his predecessor, his book is essentially based on an earlier manual by Everard Digby, *On the Art of Swimming* (*De arte natandi libri duo quorum prior regulas ipsius artis, posterior vero praxin demonstrationemque continet*) that had been published in London in 1587. (See, for example, Figure 1.5.) Digby had written in Latin. In order to reach a wider audience than only those who could read Latin, Christopher Middleton published an abridged English translation in 1595: *A Short Introduction for to learne to Swimme.*[6] Franklin does not give any indication that he knew about or had read Digby in either Latin or English. Nevertheless he certainly had devoured Thévenot, whose manual continued to be a major influence on his swimming.

The positions described in these early manuals include swimming with one foot up, or both feet raised, or one or both arms up, or both arms and legs above water. Franklin boasted that he could swim in all of these positions and added some of his own, "aiming at the graceful and easy, as well as the Useful" (A 49). (For master swimmers nowadays swimming

---

[6] See further Scott Cleary, "The Ethos Aquatic: Benjamin Franklin and the Art of Swimming," *Early American Literature* 46, no. 1 (2011): 51–67.

with just one arm or leg up constitutes an awkward practice drill; these positions definitely slow down the back crawl.)[7] The front crawl—nowadays the standard stroke—was not yet popular among Europeans and Anglo-Americans, though Africans and Native Americans were thought to be quite skilled at it. The crawl requires immersing one's head in the water. Evidently this was not a deterrent to the Africans and Native Americans, but Europeans and Anglo-Americans preferred to keep their eyes dry. Goggles had been invented but they were not much used.[8]

In 1726 the merchant Thomas Denham invited Franklin to work for him as a clerk with the prospect of an appointment as junior partner. In the same year Franklin turned down a tempting offer by Sir William Wyndham (Chancellor of the Exchequer, 1713–14) to open the first American swimming school in England. As Franklin wrote: "I had ... been ever delighted with this exercise." The freedom and exhilaration that the naked swimmer feels cannot be overestimated. Franklin's enthusiasm for swimming was doubtless an important part of his success in teaching the sport. He realized he could make a great deal of money by teaching swimming to British aristocrats, but he missed his home and family. News of Franklin's skill and success in teaching swimming had spread. Swimming became the means by which he effortlessly came into contact with the upper echelons of London society:

> *I now took leave of printing, as I thought, forever, and was daily employed in my new business, going about with Mr. Denham among the tradesmen to purchase various articles, and seeing them pack'd up, doing errands, calling upon workmen to dispatch, c.; and, when all was on board, I had a few days' leisure. On one of these days, I was, to my surprise, sent for by a great man I knew only by name, a Sir William Wyndham, and I waited upon him. He had heard by some means or other of my swimming from Chelsea to Blackfryars, and of my teaching Wygate and another young man to swim in a few hours. He had two sons, about to set out on their travels; he wish'd to have them first taught swimming, and proposed to gratify me handsomely if I would teach them. They were not yet come to town, and my stay was uncertain, so I could not undertake it; but, from this incident, I thought it likely that, if I were to remain in England and open a swimming-school, I might get a good deal of money; and it struck me so strongly, that, had the overture been sooner made me, probably I should not so soon have returned to America. After many years, you[9] and*

---

[7] Lynn Sherr, personal communication, June 23, 2018.

[8] International Swimming Hall of Fame, "The History of Goggles." https://www.ishof.org/assets/the-history-of-swimming-goggles.pdf.

[9] The *Autobiography* is addressed to Franklin's son William Franklin.

I had something of more importance to do with one of these sons of Sir William Wyndham, become Earl of Egremont, which I shall mention in its place. (A 40[10])

Franklin was in good health due to diet and exercise. He was proud of his physique (which can be attributed to swimming). Being nude apparently did not embarrass him at all, and he continued to swim even when he was eighty years old. Swimming in cold water was fashionable in the seventeenth and eighteenth centuries, but, as usual, Franklin was an independent thinker: in his fifties he preferred to take "air baths" naked in front of the window at his lodging on Craven Street, London (Figure 1.9).

In his writings over the years, Franklin discusses the effects of bathing in cold water. In the following letter it is clear that he prefers cold air baths to cold-water bathing. His preference for sleeping with the windows open is well known because of his disagreement with John Adams over the ventilation when they shared a bedroom. As he admits in a letter to his devoted friend the physician and scientist Jacques Barbeu-Dubourg, his cold air baths may not enhance his health, but they are relaxing.[11] Cold air baths may be categorized as another of Franklin's innovations: it is likely that he did not find many who adopted this practice.

From Benjamin Franklin to Jacques Barbeu-Dubourg, 28 July 1768.

Extract reprinted from *The American Museum, or, Universal Magazine*, viii (July 1790), 120.

London, July 21 [28],[12] 1768.

I will take occasion from it, to mention a practice to which I have accustomed myself. You know the cold bath has long been in vogue here as a tonic; but the shock of the cold water has always appeared to me, generally speaking, as too violent: and I have found it much more agreeable to my constitution, to bathe in another element, I mean cold air. With this view I rise early almost every morning, and sit in my chamber, without any clothes whatever, half an hour or an hour, according to the season, either reading or writing. This practice is not in the least painful, but on the contrary, agreeable; and if I return to bed afterwards, before I dress myself, as sometimes happens, I make a supplement to my night's rest, of one or two hours of the most pleasing sleep that can be imagined. I find no ill consequences whatever resulting from it, and that at least it does not

---

[10] See George Goodwin, *Benjamin Franklin in London* (New Haven, CT: Yale University Press: 2016), 139; and *PBF*, vol. 9, January 1, 1760, pp. 389–91, on Charles Wyndham, Lord Egremont.

[11] On Barbeu-Dubourg, see also Chapter 3.

[12] Barbeu-Dubourg, *Oeuvres de M. Franklin...*, 2 vols. (Paris, 1773), II, pp. 310–11, dates the letter July 28.

Figure 1.9 Benjamin Franklin House, London.[13]

On his first trip to London, Franklin lived in Little Britain and then moved to Duke Street (now known as "Sardinia Street" [A 95]). Returning later as an affluent gentleman from 1757 to 1775, he rented the parlor floor in the building now preserved as "Benjamin Franklin House" at 36 Craven Street. He would have taken his air baths in front of the large windows. From his lodging on Craven Street it is a very short walk to the Thames. Proximity to the river probably influenced Franklin's decision to choose this location.

---

[13] I am grateful to Eleanor Hamblen and Benjamin Franklin House for supplying this photograph.

injure my health, if it does not in fact contribute much to its preservation. I shall therefore call it for the future a bracing or tonic bath.

On July 21, 1726, when Franklin left England to sail home to Philadelphia, he was twenty years old. Because of unfavorable winds, the crossing took thirteen weeks. During this excruciatingly long voyage, Franklin kept a journal.[14]

While still in English waters, he "leaped overboard and swam round the ship to wash myself." Then, of course, he put his clothes on again. Washing in salty water without rinsing in fresh is not the best way to feel clean, but during the height of summer Franklin must have been desperate to wash off his sweat. The seawater was warm in August. In fact, Franklin must have been swimming in the Gulf Stream (see Epilogue).

When the ship was becalmed, Franklin seized the opportunity to swim.

On Saturday, August 6:

This morning we had a fair breeze for some hours, and then a calm that lasted all day. In the afternoon I leaped overboard and swam round the ship to wash myself. Saw several Porpoises this day.

On September 21:

It has been perfectly calm all this day, and very hot. I was determined to wash myself in the sea to-day, and should have done so had not the appearance of a shark, that mortal enemy to swimmers, deterred me: he seemed to be about five feet long, moves round the ship at some distance in a slow majestic manner, attended by near a dozen of those they call pilot-fish, of different sizes; the largest of them is not so big as a small mackerel, and the smallest not bigger than my little finger. (PBF, vol.1, 90)

On October 10:

We had an extraordinary fair wind all the afternoon and ran above an hundred miles up the Delaware before ten at night.

On October 11, 1726, the ship finally sailed into Delaware Bay (Figure 1.10), and Franklin arrived in Philadelphia.

---

[14] *Journal of a Voyage, 1726.* MS not found; reprinted from William Temple Franklin, Memoirs, 4th ed., I, Appendix, i–xix; also Library of Congress transcript *PBF*, vol. 1, 82.

Figure 1.10 Delaware boating party.

Drawing of a boating party on the Delaware, attributed to Benjamin Franklin. Note the initials 'BF" on the boat on the left.[15]

---

[15] I am grateful to Patrick Spero for suggesting this image, which is in the Library of the American Philosophical Society, and to Abigail Shelton for supplying the image.

Chapter 2

Why Swim?

Swimming was not only a healthy exercise, lots of fun, and an inexpensive way of staying clean, but knowing how to swim could make the difference between life and death. This knowledge was especially critical for anyone who chose to work on or around the water. Thus it was relevant to Ben Franklin, who hankered to go to sea when he was young. His yearning was so intense that even the books he read in order to improve his understanding of geometry included John Seller's *Practical Navigation* (1669) and Samuel Sturmy's *Mariner's Magazine* (1669) (A 15).

Franklin was well aware of the hazards of seafaring. Drowning was a not infrequent occurrence and he certainly heard about drownings of civilians numerous times as he was growing up. When he was 13, he was inspired to write a broadside ballad on the drowning of a lighthouse keeper, along with his wife, daughter, a servant, a slave, and a passenger, who were all aboard a little boat that went down (A 59). This ballad, Franklin's first publication, sold well, probably, at least in part, because people took a personal (if not voyeuristic) interest in such disastrous events, for they realized that they themselves were not immune to suffering a watery death. *The Boston News-Letter* described the drowning as "an awful and lamentable Providence."[1] Successive lighthouse keepers drowned soon after.

With a jarringly light touch, Franklin recorded another civilian drowning in his *Gazette* of October 16, 1729:[2]

> *And sometime last Week we are informed, that one Piles a Fidler, with his Wife, were overset in a Canoo near Newtown Creek. The good Man, 'tis said, prudently secur'd his Fiddle and let his Wife go to the Bottom.*

Shipwrecks—often with fatal consequences—were a common theme in eighteenth-century literature. Some books, such as the popular *Robinson Crusoe* (1719), were fictitious but perhaps based on a real event; some narrated actual events; and still others, which appear fanciful, have been shown to be historical. In *The Voyage of Richard Castelman* (1726), Castelman reminiscences about being aboard a ship that was wrecked off the coast of Roanoke.[3] Of the forty-one aboard, including crew and passengers, only eight survived. They owed their lives to two slaves who were strong swimmers. Castelman writes:

---

[1] 3–10 November 1718. For more information, see Ellen R. Cohn, "Benjamin Franklin and Traditional Music," in *Reappraising Benjamin Franklin: A Bicentennial Perspective*, ed. J. A. Leo Lemay (Newark: University of Delaware Press, 1993), 291–318, esp. p. 297, and 317n26.

[2] *PBF*, vol. 1.

[3] See further Hazel Wilkinson, "*The Voyage of Richard Castelman* (1726): A New Document for Transatlantic Literary Studies," *The Review of English Studies* 70, no. 295 (2019): 467–88. In "The water American," *Times Literary Supplement* (May 31, 2019): 10.

… We had two Blacks on Board … that were excellent Divers (for the Surge was so violent no one could stem the Billows but by diving) who offer'd to get with a Rope on Shore, and fasten it from the Ship to a Stump of a Tree.… I got into the Water and fast held on the Rope, and with the Assistance of one of the Negroes got some distance from the Ship; but the Waves drove back with such an Impetuosity, that I was many times in Danger of losing my Hold, so be carried into the main Sea; which had certainly come to pass, if I had not been assisted by the Black; for every time a great Sea was coming to break over us, he would cry out, *For the Lord's Sake, Masser, hold fast;* and whenever he called to me, I settled my self to receive the Force of the Waves. … At last, with much Struggling, I could feel my feet touch the Ground sometimes. … If the Negro had not dragg'd me on the Sands, … I must, after all my Struggling for Life, have resign'd my self to the Wave.[4]

Castelman's harrowing tale will have impressed upon Franklin that it was necessary for all who traveled on ships to know how to swim. Furthermore, the fact that the two slaves were strong swimmers would have suggested that either swimming was natural—for surely they had not learned by reading European swimming manuals—or they had learned how to do it in their place of origin. On the basis of the appearance of Castelman's book, it has been argued that Franklin collaborated with the author and published his book in London. They shared a love of music; Castelman particularly lamented losing his harpsichord in the wreck, and, of course, Franklin was also fond of playing the harpsichord.

In Franklin's day, it was not considered self-evident that men, such as sailors and fishermen, who spent much of their time on the water, should know how to swim. Thus sailors would drown, for scuffles and battles easily led to falling overboard or a ruthless enemy might truss up a sailor and toss him into the water. How common it was for sailors to know how to swim is unclear; there is not much information on the subject. There is no evidence that shipowners, ship captains, or naval officers either encouraged sailors to learn to swim, or the opposite. Nevertheless, whether a sailor could or could not swim was noted in court records and other official documents.[5] On the other hand, it has been surmised that the Royal Navy preferred that sailors not swim because that would enable and encourage them to desert. Furthermore, if a sailor fell overboard any attempt to swim would simply prolong his agonizing, inescapable death.[6]

---

[4] *The Voyage, Shipwreck, and Miraculous Escape of Richard Castelman, Gent. With a Description of Pennsylvania, and the City Philadelphia, &c.* (London, 1725), 319–20.

[5] Marcus Rediker, personal communication, April 14, 2019.

[6] Roger Deakin, *Waterlog. A Swimmer's Journey through Britain* (London: Chatto & Windus, 1999), 76.

Figure 2.1 "To Swim on the Belly, holding both your Hands still."

"This way of Swimming may be useful, in case ... you were forced on occasion to Swim with your hands tied behind you, or in case you were a prisoner, and your life or liberty depended on it."

Thévenot, 34–35, and plate XV.

Nevertheless, even if a man's arms or legs were bound, he could save himself if he knew how to swim. Handbooks for swimming give numerous examples of men who would have drowned through mere misfortune simply because their legs were caught in reeds, or owing to a shipwreck, or in other cases because their hands and feet had been deliberately tied up by an enemy. Yet there were ways of moving through the water when hands or feet could not be used. Hence, Thévenot's diagrams (Figures 2.1 and 2.2; see also Figure 1.3 "To Swim having the Legs tied together") showing how to swim with all or some limbs tied up or how to swim underwater to elude an enemy were not describing remote hypothetical events.

In some dangerous situations swimmers may save themselves by hiding underwater. This strategy would have been especially useful to sailors and pirates as well as to innocent victims of crimes at sea.

Figure 2.2 "The Agility of the Dolphin."

"This way teaches to defend and come up again in the water to take breath. … There are several sorts of dangers which may oblige us to take this method."

Thévenot, 60–61 and plate XXXVIII.

Travel by ship, even over short distances, was common. Passengers might find themselves unexpectedly in the water simply as a result of the weather and the natural hazards of the sea. Franklin wrote a kind of sermon or treatise about swimming in a letter to Oliver Neave (the full text of which follows), who was probably a merchant and often needed to travel by ship. Franklin points out that swimming is natural and refers disparagingly to the use of corks and bladders as a kind of floaty or life jacket used to support the nonswimmer while floating:

[Before 1769]

Dear Sir,

I Cannot be of opinion with you that 'tis too late in life for you to learn to swim. The river near the bottom of your garden affords you a most convenient place for the purpose. And as your new employment requires your being often on the water, of which you have such a dread, I think you would do well to make the trial; nothing being so likely to remove those apprehensions as the consciousness of an ability to swim to the shore, in case of an accident, or of supporting yourself in the water till a boat could come to take you up.

I do not know how far corks or bladders may be useful in learning to swim, having never seen much trial of them. Possibly they may be of service in supporting the body while you are learning what is called the stroke, or that manner of drawing in and striking out the hands and feet that is necessary to produce progressive motion. But you will be no swimmer till you can place some confidence in the power of the water to support you; I would therefore advise the acquiring that confidence in the first place; especially as I have known several who by a little of the practice necessary for that purpose, have insensibly acquired the stroke, taught as it were by nature.

Franklin did not record why he recommended using an egg as a goal in teaching the beginner to trust the buoyancy of the water. Raw eggs and hard-boiled eggs, however, are readily available everywhere and, as long as they are fresh, do not float in fresh water. Their bright color makes them easy to spot in clear water:

The practice I mean is this. Chusing a place where the water deepens gradually, walk coolly into it till it is up to your breast, then turn around, your face to the shore, and throw an egg into the water between you and the shore. It will sink to the bottom, and be easily seen there, as your water is clear. It must lie in water so deep as that you cannot reach it to take it up but by diving for it. To encourage yourself in undertaking to do this, reflect that your progress will be from deeper to shallower water, and that at any time you may by bringing your legs under you and standing on the bottom, raise your head far above the water. Then plunge under it with your eyes open, throwing yourself towards the egg, and endeavouring by the action of your hands and feet against the water to get forward till within reach of it. In this attempt you will find, that the water buoys you up against your inclination; that it is not so easy a thing to sink as you imagined; that you cannot, but by active force, get down to the egg. Thus you feel the power of the water to support you, and learn to confide in that power; while your endeavours to overcome it and to reach the egg teach you the manner of acting on the water with your feet and hands, which action is afterwards used in swimming to support your head higher above water, or to go forward through it.

Franklin's directions to the beginning swimmer work best if the swimmer stands upright and, feeling the support of the water, then ducks down and searches for the egg.

I would the more earnestly press you to the trial of this method, because, though I think I satisfyed you that your body is lighter than water, and that you might float in it a long time with your mouth free for breathing, if you would put yourself in a proper posture, and would be still and forbear struggling; yet till you have obtained this experimental confidence in the water, I cannot depend on your having the necessary presence of mind to recollect that posture and the directions I gave you relating to it. The surprize may put all out of your mind. For though we value ourselves on being reasonable knowing creatures, reason and knowledge seem on such occasions to be of little use to us; and the brutes to whom we allow scarce a glimmering of either, appear to have the advantage of us.

The "brutes" to whom Franklin refers are animals. He is correct, in general: most mammals with which he was familiar can swim naturally. Franklin could not have known that the giraffe, for example, can swim, but finds it difficult to find its balance in water.

I will, however, take this opportunity of repeating those particulars to you, which I mentioned in our last conversation, as by perusing them at your leisure, you may possibly imprint them so in your memory as on occasion to be of some use to you.

In some of Thévenot's diagrams the belly is quite rounded (see Figure 1.3) and looks inflated like a balloon. These illustrations exaggerate and draw attention to the need to continue to breathe deeply as well as to the buoyancy of the body, which Franklin emphasizes in his discussion.

That though the legs, arms and head, of a human body, being solid parts, are specifically something heavier than fresh water, yet the trunk, particularly the upper part from its hollowness, is so much lighter than water, as that the whole of the body taken together is too light to sink wholly under water, but some part will remain above, until the lungs become filled with water, which happens from drawing water into them instead of air, when a person in the fright attempts breathing while the mouth and nostrils are under water.

Swimming as a boy in a saltwater pond that the authorities flushed out occasionally and then in freshwater rivers, Franklin readily observed that the body was more buoyant in salt water than in fresh water:

That the legs and arms are specifically lighter than salt-water, and will be supported by it, so that a human body would not sink in salt-water, though the lungs were filled as above, but from the greater specific gravity of the head.

Using the breaststroke is tiring. Instead, if a swimmer were forced to
stay in the water for a long time, Franklin recommended floating on the back:

*That therefore a person throwing himself on his back in salt-water, and
extending his arms, may easily lie so as to keep his mouth and nostrils
free for breathing; and by a small motion of his hands may prevent turning,
if he should perceive any tendency to it.*

*That in fresh water, if a man throws himself on his back, near the
surface, he cannot long continue in that situation but by proper action of
his hands on the water. If he uses no such action, the legs and lower part
of the body will gradually sink till he comes into an upright position, in
which he will continue suspended, the hollow of the breast keeping the
head uppermost.*

*But if in this erect position, the head is kept upright above the
shoulders, as when we stand on the ground, the immersion will, by the
weight of that part of the head that is out of water, reach above the mouth
and nostrils, perhaps a little above the eyes, so that a man cannot long
remain suspended in water with his head in that position.*

*The body continuing suspended as before, and upright, if the head
be leaned quite back, so that the face looks upwards, all the back part of
the head being then under water, and its weight consequently in a great
measure supported by it, the face will remain above water quite free for
breathing, will rise an inch higher every inspiration, and sink as much
every expiration, but never so low as that the water may come over the mouth.*

*If therefore a person unacquainted with swimming, and falling acci-
dentally into the water, could have presence of mind sufficient to avoid
struggling and plunging, and to let the body take this natural position, he
might continue long safe from drowning till perhaps help would come.
For as to the cloathes, their additional weight while immersed is very
inconsiderable, the water supporting it; though when he comes out of the
water, he would find them very heavy indeed.*

*But, as I said before, I would not advise you or any one to depend
on having this presence of mind on such an occasion, but learn fairly to
swim; as I wish all men were taught to do in their youth; they would, on
many occurrences, be the safer for having that skill, and on many more
the happier, as freer from painful apprehensions of danger, to say nothing
of the enjoyment in so delightful and wholesome an exercise. Soldiers
particularly should, methinks, all be taught to swim; it might be of frequent
use either in surprising an enemy, or saving themselves. And if I had now
boys to educate, I should prefer those schools (other things being equal)*

where an opportunity was afforded for acquiring so advantageous an art,
which once learnt is never forgotten. I am, Sir, &c.

B. F.

Pirates were also a constant threat, but a person who could swim at
least had a chance of escape from a ship when they attacked. At the age
of thirteen Franklin had written a broadside ballad about "Blackbeard the
Pirate" (A 59). Blackbeard (Figure 2.3) was a famous pirate named Edward
Teach. The following two stanzas are part of a longer poem probably written
by Franklin, or by one of his contemporaries:[7]

When the Act of Grace appeared,
Captain Teach with all his Men,
Unto Carolina steered, Where they
kindly us'd him then;
There he marry'd to a Lady, And
gave her five hundred Pound,
But to her he prov'd unsteady, for he
Soon march'd off the Ground.

And returned, as I tell you, To his
Robbery as before,
Burning, sinking Ships of value,
Filling them with Purple Gore;
When he was at Carolina, There the
Governor did send
To the Governor of Virginia, that he
Might assistance lend.

Despite the obvious advantages of knowing how to swim, there were
also disadvantages. In fact, Franklin had to resist a fatal stigma going back
to antiquity that attached to floating and swimming. In parts of the American
colonies, swimming on Sunday was against the law, perhaps because the
nudity, rowdiness, and potential danger were disruptive to the Sabbath.[8]

Pliny the Elder wrote in the first century A.D. about a tribe in Scythia
who had magical powers: they would not sink in water even if their clothing
weighed them down (*NH* vii.2). The implication is that this characteristic
was demonic and barbaric. The ordeal of ducking was used until modern
times to detect witches (Figure 2.4). Those suspected of practicing witchcraft

---

[7] Ellen R. Cohn, "Benjamin Franklin and Traditional Music," in Lemay, ed., *Reapprising Benjamin Franklin,*
297–99, citing *The Worcestershire Garland: Compos'd of Three Excellent New Songs* (Newcastle, 1765).
[8] Scott Cleary, "The Ethos Aquatic: Benjamin Franklin and the Art of Swimming," *Early American Literature*
46, no. 1 (2011): 51–67.

Figure 2.3 B. Cole, *Blackbeard the pirate*, engraving, 1725.

Rare Book and Special Collections Division, Prints and Photographs Division of the Library of Congress Online Catalog. Available at https://www.loc.gov/item/2007677050/.

Figure 2.4 *Late Witch Ducking in Bedfordshire.*

"An old woman of about 60 years of age had long lain under an imputation of witchcraft.... The parish officers promised her a guinea if she should sink.... The woman was tied up in a wet sheet, all but her face and hands; her toes were tied close together, as were also her thumbs, and her hands tied to the small of her legs.... Unhappily for the poor creature, she floated.... Upon this there was a confus'd cry. " 'A witch! A witch! Drown her! Hang her.' "

"Late Witch Ducking in Bedfordshire," *The Monthly Chronologer*, July 12, 1737.
http://www.strangehistory.net/2015/10/26/late-witch-ducking-in-bedfordshire.

---

were tested by being ducked in the water trussed up like a lamb on a spit with their hands tied to their feet. If they sank, they proved their innocence, but if they floated, they were judged guilty and handed over to the authorities for punishment.

The witch trials of 1692 in Salem, Massachusetts, remain infamous today. Born in 1706, Franklin must have heard about them. He will also have learned about witch trials when he went to England, where ordeals involving ducking were more common than in the American colonies. On October 22, 1730, "A Witch Trial at Mount Holly," criticizing witchcraft as fraud, was printed in *The Pennsylvania Gazette.* It was not signed, but most editors and biographers believe that Franklin wrote it:[9]

> ... *"The Accusers being very positive that if the Accused were weighed in Scales against a Bible, the Bible would prove too heavy for them; or that if they were bound and put into the River, they would swim. ... The Accusers and the rest of the Mob ... would have the Trial by Water; accordingly a most solemn Procession was made to the Mill-pond; where both Accused and Accusers being stripp'd (saving only to the Women their shifts) were bound Hand and Foot, and severally placed in the Water, lengthways, from the Side of a Barge or Flat, having for Security only a Rope about the Middle of each, which was held by some in the Flat. The Accuser Man being thin and spare, with some Difficulty began to sink at last; but the rest every one of them swam very light upon the Water. A Sailor in the Flat jump'd out upon the Back of the Man accused, thinking to drive him down to the Bottom, but the Person bound, without any Help, came up some time before the other. The Woman Accuser, being told she did not sink, would be duck'd a second Time; when she swam again as light as before. Upon which she declared, That she believed the Accused had be-witched her to make her so light, and that she would be duck'd again a Hundred Times, but she would duck the Devil out of her. The accused Man, being surpriz'd at his own Swimming, was not so confident of his Innocence as before, but said, If I am a Witch, it is more than I know. The more thinking Part of the Spectators were of Opinion, that any Person so bound and plac'd in the Water (unless they were mere Skin and Bones) would swim till their Breath was gone, and their Lungs fill'd with Water. But it being the general Belief of the Populace that the Womens Shifts, and the Garters with which they were bound help'd to support them; it is said they are to be tried again the next warm Weather, naked."*

---

[9] Original source *PBF*, vol. 1, 182–83. https://founders.Archives.gov/documents/Franklin/01-01-02-0056.

Figure 2.5 Robert Feke, *Benjamin Franklin*, ca. 1746.

First portrait of Benjamin Franklin, age 40. Here Franklin looks hale and hearty, his complexion healthy and his body sturdy, but with no excessive plumpness. He is, in short, an advertisement for the beneficial effects of swimming (see p. 27 passim). The background at right showing mountains and clouds alludes to Franklin's interest in natural philosophy. In terms of the styles of the time, his wig and clothing are plain.[10]

Fogg Art Museum, Harvard University. Harvard University Portrait Collection, Bequest of Dr. John Collins Warren, 1856. Accession Number H47.

---

[10] For further information, see Wayne Craven, "The American and British Portraits of Benjamin Franklin," in *Reappraising Benjamin Franklin. A Bicentennial Perspective*, ed. J. A. Leo Lemay (Newark: University of Delaware Press, 1993), 247–71, esp. pp. 249–51.

Chapter 3

Swimming in France

Figure 3.1 Alexis-Nicolas Pérignon, *l'hôtel de Valentinois (courtyard)*, 1775–80.

Paris: Musée Carnavalet, Histoire de Paris. https://www.parismuseescollections.paris.fr/fr/musee-carnavalet/
oeuvres/vue-de-l-hotel-de-valentinois-du-cote-cour-a-passy-vers-1775-1780#infos-secondaires-detail
D.16366.

When Benjamin Franklin came to France on official government business in 1776, he spent two months in Paris and then moved to Passy, a district in the west of Paris, where it was possible to swim in the Seine. He lived in a wing of the lavish home of Jacques-Donatien Le Ray de Chaumont known as *l'hôtel de Valentinois* (Figure 3.1), which was located on the shore of the river. Passy was approximately three and a half miles from central Paris, less than an hour's ride in a two-horse carriage. Because the estate bordered on the Seine, Franklin and his visitors could also travel by boat.[1]

Franklin brought two grandsons with him to France. William Temple Franklin (1760–1823, known as "Temple") was the son of Franklin's son

---

[1] See further Miriam Simon et al., *Benjamin Franklin: un américain à Paris (1776–1785)*. Musée Carnavalet. Histoire de Paris, 5 décembre 2007–9 mars 2008. Paris: Paris Musées, 2007.

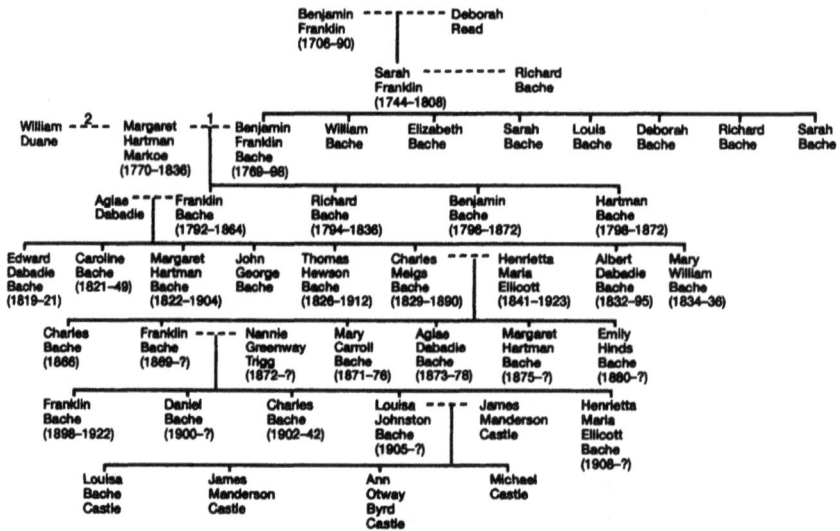

Figure 3.2 Benjamin Franklin's family tree.

The genealogical chart compiled by one of the descendants of Benjamin Franklin and Deborah Read omits Temple, but Benny refers to him in his journal as his cousin.[2]

American Philosophical Society.

William Franklin and an unknown woman, and Benjamin Franklin Bache (1769–1798, known as "Benny") was the son of his daughter, Sally (Sarah), and her husband, Richard (Figures 3.2 and 3.5). Having lost his only legitimate son, Francis, at the age of four, Franklin must have considered these grandsons especially dear. Temple served as a secretary to his grandfather. Benny attended school in Paris for two years, after which his grandfather sent him to Geneva because he did not want Benny to continue to be educated in monarchical France.

Franklin did travel often from Passy to Paris for a proper bath (doubtless especially when it was too cold to swim) and for secret meetings with other diplomats and politicians. The cabins for bathing were private and therefore a visitor would need to ask the staff if a particular gentleman was present. Franklin made arrangements to meet the British politician and physician Benjamin Vaughan (1751–1835) at the baths of Poitevin (a floating bathhouse with 22 private rooms for bathing, established March 13, 1761, at the foot of the Pont de la Tournelle, facing the Quai Dauphin).

Franklin concludes his meeting with the not very subtle suggestion to his younger friend that he could use the occasion to take a bath himself.

> To Benjamin Vaughan
> Thursday, Sept. 18, 1777
>
> *I shall be very happy to see my dear Friend if it may be without Inconvenience to him; and the sooner the happier. The Duke de Chaulnes, who was with me last Night, has ask'd me to dine with him on Sunday, when he expected you: But that is a long time for me to wait; And I cannot think of another Place where a Meeting with me would not occasion Speculation. Yes: There is les Bains de Poitevin a large white wooden Building upon a Boat in the River opposite to the Tuilleries. You may go there in a Hackney Coach; and you will find me there at Six in the Evening precisely. The People know me only by Sight as I go there often to bathe. Ask for an old Englishman with grey Hair. It is the Evening of this Thursday that I mean: But if you are otherwise engag'd, name your Hour of Tomorrow, and I will make it suit me. Yours most affectionately.*[2]
>
> *You may come there an Hour sooner as to take the Bath your self if agreable: I shall be there at 5.*
>
> *Addressed:* A Monsr / Monsieur Vaughan / Hotel des Bains de Bourbon / Rue Richelieu / à Paris

Franklin's friend Abbé Lefebvre de la Roche[3] observed that Franklin swam in the Seine at Passy very early in the morning. In his old age Franklin called himself "Old Fatsides, " but he would not have had to be concerned about a large audience gathering to watch him swim nude in the Seine at daybreak. He was probably accompanied by just one servant and by a grandson.

Like many carefully brought-up children, Benny Franklin kept a journal. Because he was educated in France and Geneva he wrote in French.[4] An English version of his notebooks translated by one of his descendants is now in the Library of the American Philosophical Society.[5] Benny probably had learned to swim in the Delaware River; doubtless he

---

[2] *PBF*, vol. 25, 539.

[3] "Note sur Franklin," 1790. Gilbert Chinard, "Recollections of Benjamin Franklin," *Proceedings of the American Philosophical Society* 94 (1950): 220.

[4] The French version was translated by Benny's granddaughter Margaret Hartman Bache. She refers to it as a "Diary."

[5] The quotations in the present book are transcribed from this English version and include the punctuation marks used there.

also swam in Lake Geneva—which is still a favorite destination for swimming. He left a record of swimming in the Seine. Benny's journal entries from the warm months give brief reports about dining and social events, but they are replete with long descriptions of swimming in the Seine and playing on the shore with kites. He reports drownings in a brief matter-of-fact way, for they were common.

Benny first mentions swimming on May 18, 1784, when he was 15 years old. On the same day a servant, who apparently did not know how to swim, drowned:

> *In returning from bathing,[6] which I have done everyday for about a week I met one of the house servants who asked me if I was not returning from bathing. I replied joking "One cannot bathe it is too cold." His friends however dragged him to the river where he had no desire to go, and falling into a hole he had drowned.*

Apparently the hole had not been fixed or fenced-off.

May 19, 1784

> *Another man had been drowned today in the same spot as our domestic.*

Benny Bache knew John Quincy Adams, for they attended school together in Paris. In a journal entry dated August 10, 1783, John Quincy mentions visiting Passy.[7] Although by the time John Quincy became president he was famous as a devoted swimmer, there is no evidence that he swam with Benny in Paris. John Quincy was two years older than Benny. Benny, however, frequently mentions his friend Alexander, the son of one of Franklin's friends. The boys were constant companions: Benny details their numerous activities, including swimming and playing with kites in Passy. The vagaries of kite-flying on the shores of the Seine often preceded a swim.

July 19, 1784

> *With Alexander I have constructed a kite five feet in height.*

---

[6] *[M]e baigner*. The context makes it clear that Benny swam (rather than bathing in a tub).

[7] For further information, see James Tagg, *Benjamin Franklin Bache and the Philadelphia Aurora* (Philadelphia: University of Pennsylvania Press, 1991), 28; Margaret A. Hogan, *John Quincy Adams: Life Before the Presidency*. https://millercenter.org/president/jqadams/life-before-the-presidency. I am grateful to Miriam Schneier for this reference.

We tried to fly it, but the wind was too strong for the string and it broke, as it was upon the river bank and it fell upon the other side. I undressed in haste and swam across the river but when I reached the other side, I saw some strangers who had seized it and had already carried it very far, for they were near the village of Vaugirard some distance away. They had not had the sense to take the string, out of the water so that I took it, and swam with it to the other side. The misfortune made us sad but it did not destroy all our courage so we decided to buy another string and make a kite of 7 feet, and employ a carpenter to make a walnut stake of 7 feet, and a hoop. Our preparations made me postpone the raising of it until the next day. We will make a kite of 4 feet for the little string.

July 20, 1784

We made the 7 foot kite with Williams.

July 25, 1784

We made the one of 4 feet.

July 26, 1784

We raised them both. The wind being very strong, the cord of the larger one broke, and the kite fell on the other side of the river. Alexander went after it but could find no trace of it. Not withstanding the force of the wind, the string of the 4 foot, one did not break; that is why we decided to make one of 6 feet for the string, which the 7 foot one had broken. We bought another stick and a hoop.

July 27, 1784

It was finished and ready to fly.

July 28, 1784

I tried it with Alexander, but the wind being very strong I would not let out all the cord.

September 7, 1784

Since the first of the month it has been very hot. I propose to bathe today. At 7 in the evening I bathed.[8]

Benny recorded another all-day adventure that involved crossing the Seine and returning.[9] It is difficult to calculate the distance across the

---

[8] "Je me suis baigné."
[9] Chinard, "Recollections," 220.

Figure 3.3 Charles-Léopold Grevenbroeck, *Passy and Chaillot seen from Grenelle*, 1743.

———————————————

Village of Passy. View of Grenelle with boats, carriage, horses.

Musée Carnavalet. Histoire de Paris. Salon de 1743,P 2123. https://www.parismuseescollections.paris.fr/ fr/musee-carnavalet/oeuvres/passy-et-chaillot-vus-de-grenelle.

———————————————

Seine at Passy (Figure 3.3) in the eighteenth century because in the nineteenth century the river was controlled by levees and locks that greatly narrowed it and made it deeper. Nowadays the Pont de Bir-Hakeim (also known as the the Pont de Passy) spans 204 meters (669 feet, 3 inches).[10]

The Seine was a busy river, rather dangerous for swimming. It was necessary to avoid ferries, fishing boats, and other vessels, whose skippers did not expect to find swimmers in their path. In his journal Benny mentions avoiding a galliote (a small boat with sail and oars). Alexander eventually took a ferry back across, but Benny courageously swam both ways. Both boys needed to dry their clothes when they arrived. Like his grandfather, Benny performed at least one of the feats explained in early manuals, for he swam across the river balancing his clothing on his head (Figure 3.4). (See also Figure 1.5: "Swimming while carrying things above the water.")

———————————————

[10] Jérôme Poisson, "Pont de Bir-Hakeim," in Guy Lambert, *Les Ponts de Paris* (Paris: Action artistique de la ville de Paris, 1999), 226.

Figure 3.4 "To Swim holding up your Hands."

"While you Swim on your back, it is easy to put your hands to what use you please, but it is difficult to hold them upright, and Swim at the same time too."

Thévenot, p. 50, and plate XXX facing p. 50.

September 8, 1784

After dinner Alexander and I crossed the river at the base of the mountain at Passy and fished on the opposite side; we caught nothing because the worms were not the right kind. When the time came to leave, not wishing to return by the same route by which we had come and desirous also to bathe; we undressed intending to swim across the river with our clothes on our heads. Alexander tried it but found his package too heavy. I tried and thought I could, so I set off, when ¾ across the river, I was obliged to turn back, because of the Galliote which was very near (to avoid the rope which sank in the water). I renewed my efforts and succeeded in avoiding it, by passing under it. When I was about ¾ across my package which was not very steady all the time, fell, however I pushed it to the shore swimming after it. All my clothes were wet; fortunately it was night. I put on my coat, my breeches, & my shoes, and put the rest in my handkerchief and ran home quickly and changed them. Afterward came Alexander and this is what he told me happened to him "After you left me," said he, "I remained some time longer in the water, and left to go by boat.... I dried my clothes and so went to bed."

Like his grandfather, Benny was interested in the various transformations of water. He ice-skated on the Seine, sometimes for three hours at a time. On January 1, 1785, he noted, "the river rose when the snow melted."[11]

Swimming with his grandfather and sharing Franklin's childhood fascination with kites must have been among the inspirations that prompted Benny to admire his grandfather. In a letter to Benny's mother, Sally Bache (Figure 3.5), Ben Franklin's friend Dorcas Montgomery describes Benny: "He found his G-Papa very different from other old Persons, for they were fretful and complaining, and dissatisfy'd. And my G.Papa is laughing and cheerful like a young person."[12]

There was, and still is, much gossip and speculation about Franklin's relationships with women while in France (Figure 3.6). Doubtless women admired Franklin's wit and intellect. We also suppose that his strong physique and good hygiene contributed to his attractiveness, even at an advanced age. His uniqueness among the dandified Frenchmen added to his allure.

Paris also offered Franklin an opportunity to discuss theories of swimming. He met a new friend, Jacques Barbeu-Dubourg (1709–79), around 1767.[13] Barbeu-Dubourg, a physician, scientist, and philosopher, translated into French the fourth edition of Franklin's *Collected Works*, adding his own writing.[14] The books contained some of Franklin's letters, including the one in which he praises nude air baths (July 28, 1768, see Chapter 1). Barbeu-Dubourg nowadays appears to be a minor figure in the galaxy of eighteenth-century French intellectuals. He was, however, a great admirer of Franklin, who, in turn, managed to procure admission to the American Philosophical Society for him. Barbeu-Dubourg discussed many topics of interest to Franklin, including lightning rods. His faithful translation of Franklin's letter to O. Naeve on swimming took five pages (pp. 241–46).[15] Barbeu-Dubourg continued the discussion of swimming for

---

[11] See further Claude-Anne Lopez and Eugenia W. Herbert, *The Private Franklin* (New York: Norton, 1985), 270.

[12] Letter from Dorcas Montgomery to Sarah Franklin Bache, July 26, 1783, Bache Family Papers, B 812 1, Series I Correspondence. The Montgomery letter is cited in *PBF*, volume 40: May 16 through September 15, 1783, 390n5: Benjamin Franklin to Richard and Sarah Bache, Passy, July 27, 1783. I am grateful to Tracey de Jong for suggesting this reference.

[13] Name as spelled in Gallica. In some publications he is "Barbeau-Dubourg." For more information, see Alfred Owen Aldridge, "Jacques Barbeu-Dubourg, a French Disciple of Benjamin Franklin," *Proceedings of the American Philosophical Society* 95, no. 4 (Aug. 17, 1951): 331–92.

[14] Jacques Barbeu-Dubourg, ed., *Œuvres de M. Franklin, docteur ès loix … traduites de l'anglois sur la quatrième édition, avec des additions nouvelles figures en taille* (2 vols., Paris, 1773).

[15] The full text in English of Franklin's letter to Naeve appears in Chapter 2.

Figure 3.5 John Hoppner, *Mrs. Richard Bache (Sarah Franklin, 1743–1808)*, 1793.

Sally has the same prominent round chin as her mother, Deborah (see Figure 1.7).

Metropolitan Museum of Art. Catharine Lorillard Wolfe Collection, Wolfe Fund, 1901. Accession number 01.20. Image copyright © The Metropolitan Museum of Art. Image source: Art Resource, NY. ART396491

---

another eleven pages in the form of a letter to Franklin dated February 12, 1773 (pp. 247–257). Barbeu-Dubourg opens his composition by stating that he did some research in the *Dictionnaire Encyclopédique* and found

Figure 3.6 Portrait by workshop of Joseph Siffred Duplessis. *Benjamin Franklin in France*, around 1779.

For his portrait, Franklin dressed simply in a red suede waistcoat with a fur collar. In contrast to his French friends, he did not advertise the latest fashion: he did not wear a wig, lace, perfume, fancy buckles, or cod piece. The gray hair mentioned in 1771 in his letter to Vaughan does not appear here. As he was representing a democracy, he did not indulge in conspicuous consumption. His pudgy face and bulging belly in this and other portraits of the period, however, betrayed his life abroad, where he attended lavish banquets and dinners lasting two hours or more. Franklin's shaggy, slightly disheveled appearance recalls that of Socrates and other earlier philosophers, whose simple dress indicated that their minds were fixed on more important matters than personal appearance.

Musée Carnavalet, Histoire de Paris, 1074. https://www.parismuseescollections.paris.fr/fr/recherche?text= Duplessis.%20franklin.

little information about swimming (p. 246). Apparently he did not consult Thévenot's manual, although it had been published in Paris in 1696 and Franklin had read it.

Barbeu-Dubourg compliments Franklin on recommending the ingenious exercise of throwing an egg in clear water and asking the beginning swimmer to fetch it (p. 252). He remarks that it is definitely easier to swim nude (p. 252). He also points out that floating is not the same as swimming, inasmuch as the latter involves movement (p. 253). In the final section Barbeu-Dubourg outlines aspects of swimming and drowning that could merit further investigation. Despite Barbeu-Dubourg's assertiveness, his piece is clearly theoretical: he does not write with the ease of someone who actually knows how to swim. In contrast, Franklin's lessons are practical and obviously based on experience. After his introduction, Barbeu-Dubourg generally uses an impersonal style well suited to his deferential manner. In contrast, Franklin prefers the first person.

From Jacques Barbeu-Dubourg

Printed in Jacques Barbeu-Dubourg, ed., *Oeuvres de M. Franklin ...* (2 vols., Paris, 1773), vol. II, 246–57.

12 Février 1773.

The following section is a summary in English of Barbeu-Dubourg's outline, which includes, in particular, the points to which Franklin responds. The complete French text can be found in the Appendix.

> I found your letter to M. Néave much too short because its excellent content made me want a lot of other things about which I never had the least idea. I went to look in the great *Dictionnaire Encyclopédique* under *nager, natation, &c.* [to swim, swimming, etc.]. I was surprised to see how little progress had been made on this topic.

Section One

The first object, in my opinion, should be to determine the weight of a cubic foot of water, plain water, and then more or less salinated.

> Then to determine the weight of a human body, weighing an adult male, then a woman, a child, an old person.

> Perhaps we will discover that some float naturally on top, some below the surface, and some sink.

II The second goal could be to consider the special structure and the different maneuvers of animals that live continually or frequently in water.

If this investigation seems too dangerous one should cover one's head with a kind of diving bell.

Section Two

We come to the principal object, that is to say what properly constitutes the art of swimming: how to stay on the surface of the water and the means of moving through it as one pleases.

It is easy to figure out what can compensate for the excess weight of our bodies in order to maintain ourselves on the surface. Gourds, bladders, bottles can help — provided their interior is empty. The diving suit of M. l'Abbé de la Chapelle is definitely superior to all that sort of thing, although I have heard talk of certain life jackets or vests invented in England.

II In the second place, properly speaking, floating on the water is not swimming: swimming implies a forward movement through the water.

III In the third place, one should compare the advantages and disadvantages of different postures in the water: the two principal ones are lying on the stomach and lying on the back.

IV In the fourth place, to foresee the accidents that can occur in water like strokes, cramps, fainting, &c.

Section Three

First consider the pleasure of bathing and of exercising in the water.

II In the second place research the usefulness of the art of swimming.

Should swimming be part of the regular education of the young?

For what professions is it particularly necessary?

III Consider in the third place the health benefits of bathing and of exercising in the water.

How hot or cold should the water be to be healthy and not harmful?

What time is it good to bathe? Before or after eating?

Must one avoid entering a very hot bath and what is the danger in doing so?

IV In the fourth place consider if it is easy to learn to swim by oneself, and how much easier it is to learn with a good teacher.

V In the fifth place give simple instructions that are easy to recall for those who happen to fall into the water without knowing how to swim.

VI In the sixth place know how to perceive that someone is in danger of drowning.

VII Consider the formal reason why people who drown die.

VIII In the eighth place everything that pertains to this subject in the ancient authors.

Inform travelers about different styles of swimming in different countries.

IX In the last place make proposals relative to this objective, principally in great cities located on rivers like Paris, London, &c.

Franklin did not respond as Barbeu-Dubourg might have hoped: he answered politely, but briefly, choosing to write about only some of the topics his friend had raised, taking them up in the same order as Barbeu-Dubourg. He adds bulk to his letter by incorporating two passages from his *Autobiography*.

To Jacques Barbeu-Dubourg

A French version was printed in Jacques Barbeu-Dubourg, ed., *Oeuvres de M. Franklin* ... (2 vols., Paris, 1773), vol. II, 258–61.[16] The following English version was published in Albert Henry Smyth, *The Writings of Benjamin Franklin* (New York, 1907), vol. V, no. 630, 542–45.

[March?, 1773] The dating is based on the fact that Franklin's letter is a response to Barbeu-Dubourg's letter.

---

[16] William B. Wilcox, ed., *PBF*, vol. 20, *January 1 through December 31, 1773* (New Haven, CT: Yale University Press, 1976), 131–33.

J'appréhende bien de ne pouvoir trouver le temps de faire sur cette matière toutes les recherches et les expériences qui seraient à désirer. Je me bornerai donc à faire ici quelques remarques....

I am apprehensive, that I shall not be able to find leisure for making all the disquisitions and experiments which would be desirable on this subject. I must, therefore, content myself with a few remarks.

The specific gravity of some human bodies, in comparison to that of water, has been examined by Mr. Robinson, in our Philosophical Transactions, Volume L., page 30, for the year 1757. He asserts, that fat persons with small bones float most easily upon the water.

The diving-bell is accurately described in our Transactions.

Franklin dismisses the diving bell and—a little further on—the diving suit because, after all, he neither invented nor used them. He was proud, however, that, as a precocious child, he had invented and experimented with swimming paddles. Here he inserts the same story about his invention of swimming paddles that was quoted in Chapter 1.

When I was a boy, I made two oval palettes, each about ten inches long, and six broad, with a hole for the thumb, in order to retain it fast in the palm of my hand. They much resembled a painter's palette. In swimming I pushed the edges of these forward, and I struck the water with their flat surfaces as I drew them back. I remember I swam faster by means of these pallets, but they fatigued my wrists. I also fitted to the soles of my feet a kind of sandals; but I was not satisfied with them, because I observed that the stroke is partly given by the inside of the feet and the ankles, and not entirely with the soles of the feet.

Franklin continues with a brief description of life vests:

We have here waistcoats for swimming, which are made of double sail-cloth, with small pieces of cork quilted in between them.

I know nothing of the scaphandre *[diving suit] of M. de la Chapelle.*

I know by experience, that it is a great comfort to a swimmer, who has a considerable distance to go, to turn himself sometimes on his back, and to vary in other respects the means of procuring a progressive motion.

When he is seized with the cramp in the leg, the method of driving it away is, to give to the parts affected a sudden, vigorous and violent shock; which he may do in the air as he swims on his back.

Franklin here recommends raising the cramped leg in the air—a postion described by Thévenot. This maneuver, however (as swimmers nowadays can attest), could well have increased the severity of the cramp.

Franklin displays here, as elsewhere, his intense interest in temperatures that are favorable and unfavorable for swimming.

> *During the great heats of summer there is no danger in bathing, however warm we may be, in rivers which have been thoroughly warmed by the sun. But to throw one's self into cold spring water, when the body has been heated by exercise in the sun, is an imprudence which may prove fatal. I once knew an instance of four young men, who, having worked a harvest in the heat of the day, with a view of refreshing themselves plunged into a spring of cold water; two died upon the spot, a third the next morning, and the fourth recovered with great difficulty. A copious draught of cold water, in similar circumstances, is frequestly attended with the same effect in North America.*

The dramatic anecdote Franklin relates to prove his point seems exaggerated and most unlikely. Nevertheless the multiple deaths might have occurred if there had been a confluence of unusual circumstances. Because it was harvest time [probably in the fall] and the men were overheated, the water pooled up in the spring could have been very cold only if it was continually fed by a very cold underground source: but it would not have been close to freezing. Even in water as cold as 32.5–40°F exhaustion or unconsciousness does not occur instantly, but takes 15–30 minutes.[17] Therefore two men would not have "died upon the spot" unless they simultaneously suffered a heart attack. One man survived because cold water does not automatically kill every person; in fact some swimmers enjoy it (see Epilogue). Therefore it is possible that although the dead men were "young," they had pre-existing maladies that rendered them vulnerable to the sudden shock of cold water and unable to climb out of the spring.[18] Or perhaps they did not know that the spring was deep and they did not know how to swim.

After discussing the three deaths, Franklin ends with a grand finale, summing up the health benefits of swimming. His personal experience of the effect of swimming on diarrhea and constipation is not confirmed as a common result by modern medical authorities.

> *The exercise of swimming is one of the most healthy and agreeable in the world. After having swam for an hour or two in the evening, one sleeps*

---

[17] U.S. Search and Rescue Task Force, "Cold Water Survival." www.ussartf.org/cold_water_survival.htm.

[18] I am grateful to Dr. Sanford Friedman for comments on the effects of extreme cold on swimmers.

coolly the whole night, even during the most ardent heat of summer. Perhaps, the pores being cleansed, the insensible perspiration increases and occasions this coolness. It is certain that much swimming is the means of stopping a diarrhoea, and even of producing a constipation. With respect to those, who do not know how to swim, or who are affected with a diarrhoea at a season which does not permit them to use that exercise, a warm bath, by cleansing and purifying the skin, is found very salutary, and often effects a radical cure. I speak from my own experience, frequently repeated, and that of others, to whom I have recommended this.

You will not be displeased if I conclude these hasty remarks by informing you, that as the ordinary method of swimming is reduced to the act of rowing with the arms and legs, and is consequently a laborious and fatiguing operation when the space of water to be crossed is considerable; there is a method in which a swimmer may pass to great distances with much facility, by means of a sail. This discovery I fortunately made by accident, and in the following manner.

Franklin takes the opportunity to boast again about a precocious invention (also discussed in Chapter 1).

When I was a boy, I amused myself one day with flying a paper kite; and approaching the bank of a pond, which was near a mile broad, I tied the string to a stake, and the kite ascended to a very considerable height above the pond, while I was swimming. In a little time, being desirous of amusing myself with my kite, and enjoying at the same time the pleasure of swimming, I returned; and, loosing from the stake the string with the little stick which was fastened to it, went again into the water, where I found, that, lying on my back and holding the stick in my hands, I was drawn along the surface of the water in a very agreeable manner. Having then engaged another boy to carry my clothes round the pond, to a place which I pointed out to him on the other side, I began to cross the pond with my kite, which carried me quite over without the least fatigue, and with the greatest pleasure imaginable. I was only obliged occasionally to halt a little in my course, and resist its progress, when it appeared that, by following too quick, I lowered the kite too much; by doing which occasionally I made it rise again.

Inspired by Barbeu-Dubourg's references to Paris and London, Franklin closes his letter lightheartedly:

I have never since that time practiced this singular mode of swimming, though I think it not impossible to cross in this manner from Dover to Calais. The packet-boat, however, is still preferable.

Je n'ai point pratiqué depuis ce temps cette méthode singulière de nager, mais j'imagine qu'un homme pourroit au besoin traverser ainsi à la nage de Douvre à Calais. Cependant une barque vaut encore mieux.[19]

---

[19] Jacques Barbeu-Dubourg, ed., *Oeuvres de M. Franklin...* (2 vols., Paris, 1773), II, 258–61. 626193 = 020-131a.html.

When Franklin and Barbeu-Dubourg were exchanging letters, swimming was becoming more popular in France. In 1785, Barthélémy Turquin founded the first swimming school in a floating basin on the Seine and in 1790 published a proposal to establish public swimming schools.[20] This four-page document includes suggestions for a sliding scale of fees. Moreover, special efforts were to be made to teach swimming to men who drove wagons and coaches. Oddly enough, he does not include sailors or boatmen in his recommendation. The provision concerning coachmen was added because wagons and coaches often drove on a path next to bodies of water or even through the water where they might pick up passengers from ships (Figure 3.7). Drivers who could swim would be able to save themselves and their passengers from drowning. A special fund was to be established to support widows whose husbands had died while performing public service on a river. More swimming schools began to appear in France at the end of the eighteenth century.[21]

Franklin influenced the development of swimming in France, as well as in England and America. His most extensive writing about swimming became available in French. His authority in the field of swimming continued even after he had left Paris and died. Gallica, the digital library created by the Bibliothèque nationale de France, cites *L'art de nager, d'après les préceptes de B. Franklin, G. Feydel et autres* (Paris, 1826). On his opening pages (pp. 3–4) the author, identified only as "L. L. K.," refers to Franklin's letter to Neave. He faithfully describes Franklin's method of teaching by tossing an egg into the water and trusting the buoyancy of the water to support the swimmer (pp. 50–53).

Franklin continued to be an authority in the field of swimming.[22] For example, William Buchan (1728–1805) titles his work *New Art of Swimming: with Dr. Franklin's Directions to Swimmers, and Dr. Buchan's Advice on River & Sea-Bathing* (London: A. Lemoine, 1798; Figure 3.8). Buchan (p. iv) lists Thévenot and Franklin among only four swimming experts. Franklin's writing was sometimes plagiarized with no credit given.[23] Nevertheless, he was the authority who was most often mentioned in discussions

---

[20] Barthélémy Turquin, *Projet d'une école de natation en faveur de la garde bourgeoise nationale de Paris* (Paris, impr. de Valleyre aîné, 1790).

[21] For more information, see Isabelle Duhau, "Les baignades en rivière d'Île-de-France, des premiers aménagements à la piscine parisienne Joséphine-Baker, *Livraisons de l'histoire de l'architecture* 14 (2007): 9–38. Also published as Isabelle Duhau, "Les baignades en rivière d'Île-de-France, des premiers aménagements à la piscine parisienne Joséphine-Baker," Livraisons de l'histoire de l'architecture [En ligne], 14 2007, mis en ligne le 10 décembre 2009, consulté le 19 novembre 2018. https://doi.org/10.4000/lha.422.

[22] For more information, see Ralph Thomas, *Swimming. With Lists of Books Published in English German French And Other European Languages And Critical Remarks On The Theory And Practice Of Swimming And Resuscitation Biography History Bibliography Including Upwards Of One Hundred Illustrations* (London: Sampson, Low, Marston & Co., 1904, reprint London: Forgotten Books, 2016), 16.

[23] Buchan, *New Art of Swimming*, 54.

FRONTISPIECE.

SEA BATHING.

Figure 3.7 Horse-drawn coaches in a river.

William Buchan, *New Art of Swimming: with Dr. Franklin's Directions to Swimmers, and Dr. Buchan's Advice on River & Sea-Bathing*, frontispiece (London, 1798). https://catalog.hathitrust.org/Record/100163697.marcBabel.hathitrust.org.

---

of swimming, usually positively, but sometimes critically, and at times through false attributions. He was credited with advocating the sidestroke for advancing swiftly through water, but this attribution was false.[24] In the exchange of letters between Franklin and Barbeu-Dubourg neither mentions sidestroke (which can be a less-tiring, long-distance stroke). Although the

---

[24] Thomas, *Swimming*, 287–88.

Figure 3.8 Swimming manual shows Franklin as first author.

William Buchan, *New Art of Swimming: with Dr. Franklin's Directions to Swimmers, and Dr. Buchan's Advice on River & Sea-Bathing* (London: A. Lemoine, 1798). See also Figure 3.7.

---

sidestroke is illustrated in Thévenot's manual, it was not much used in Europe and Anglo-America until the nineteenth century.[25] Thévenot's description of the stroke is vague and not well thought out.[26] The lack of clear instructions for the sidestroke is probably due, at least in part, to the fact that the movements are not symmetrical and thus difficult to

---

[25] Thévenot, 32–33 and plate XIV.
[26] Thévenot, 32–33 and plate XIV.

describe and teach: Each arm and each leg has a distinctive movement and these are reversed if the swimmer changes sides. Furthermore, what is nowadays referred to as the "scissors kick" had not yet been perfected.

Whether a person who felt hot should plunge into cold water continued to be controversial: Franklin was cited on both sides of this debate.[27] Moreover, Franklin's lesson using the tossed egg was frequently the focus of criticism.[28] Some would-be authorities (who obviously had never tried it), asserted that human beings could not see under water.[29]

Franklin was most unusual among savants in his lifelong attention to swimming.[30] Our survey of swimming in England and France indicates that, in Franklin's era, swimming evolved from an upper-class skill, with a swimming manual written in Latin and lessons available for a fee, to a more widespread democratized practice. Franklin's authority and evangelical writing about swimming were powerful influences in popularizing this art in the Western world.

---

[27] Thomas, *Swimming*, 90.
[28] Thomas, *Swimming*, 304.
[29] Thomas, *Swimming*, 155–56, 221.
[30] Thomas, *Swimming*, 21.

Epilogue

Water, Water, Everywhere

Benjamin Franklin is more famous for his scientific investigations than for his swimming. Personal experience gained by swimming in a variety of bodies of water—fresh and salt, rivers, ocean, and landlocked—doubtless helped to foster his interest in the behavior and characteristics of water. In 1726, on his first voyage from London to Philadelphia, Franklin kept a journal noting the winds, currents, weather, celestial phenomena, other ships, vegetation, and sea creatures, including porpoises and tiny crabs. He was also interested in the behavior of human beings, both in the water and afloat on it in ships.

September 23, 1726[1]

There is really something strangely cheering to the spirits in the meeting of a ship at sea, containing a society of creatures of the same species and in the same circumstances with ourselves, after we had been long separated and excommunicated as it were from the rest of mankind.

Franklin found it difficult to distinguish the ocean fauna from the flora in which they were embedded. He recorded his daily observations.

September 28, 1726

This afternoon we took up several branches of gulf weed (with which the sea is spread all over from the Western Isles to the coast of America); but one of these branches had something peculiar in it. In common with the rest it had a leaf about three quarters of an inch long, indented like a saw, and a small yellow berry filled with nothing but wind; besides which it bore a fruit of the animal kind, very surprising to see. It was a small shell-fish like a heart, the stalk by which it proceeded from the branch being partly of a gristly kind. Upon this one branch of the weed there were nearly forty of these vegetable animals; the smallest of them near the end contained a substance somewhat like an oyster, but the larger were visibly animated, opening their shells every moment, and thrusting out a set of unformed claws, not unlike those of a crab; but the inner part was still a kind of soft jelly. Observing the weed more narrowly, I spied a very small crab crawling among it, about as big as the head of a ten-penny nail, and of a yellowish colour, like the weed itself. This gave me some reason to think that he was a native of the branch, that he had not long since been in the same condition with the rest of these little embrios that appeared in the shells, this being the method of their generation; and that consequently all the time spent

---

[1] The following excerpts from the *Journal* are quoted from Joyce E. Chaplin, ed., *Benjamin Franklin's Autobiography* (New York: Norton, 2012), 226–28, excerpted from *PBF*, vol. 1, 72–99.

with this odd kind of fruit might be crabs in due time. To strengthen my conjecture, I have resolved to keep the weed in salt water, renewing it every day till we come on shore, by this experiment to see whether any more crabs will be produced or not in this manner....

September 29, 1726

Upon shifting the water in which I had put the weed yesterday, I found another crab, much smaller than the former, who seemed to have newly left his habitation. But the weed begins to wither, and the rest of the embrios are dead. This new comer fully convinces me, that at least this sort of crabs are generated in this manner.

Out on the ocean in the dark with no obstructions to block his view, Franklin was able to see the moon and stars clearly. The first eclipse he mentions here is lunar; the second, a fortnight later, was solar. He does not state whether he managed to discover a means of observing the latter without injuring his eyes.

September 30, 1726

I sat up last night to observe an eclipse of the moon, which the calendar calculated for London informed us would happen at five o'clock in the morning. It began with us about eleven last night, and continued till near two this morning, darkening her body about six digits, or one half; the middle of it being about half an hour after twelve, by which we may discover that we are in a meridian of about four hours and half from London, or 67½ degrees of longitude, and consequently have not much above one hundred leagues to run. This is the second eclipse we have had within these fifteen days.... We have had abundance of dolphins about us these three or four days.

Although he had rejected the idea of starting a swimming school in England, when Franklin returned to North America he became a voluble evangelist for swimming instruction. This time he did not consider the financial advantages but rather the public weal. He advised parents to teach their children how to swim so that they would be safe and not afraid of the water. Years later when Franklin was an influential figure in Philadelphia, he advocated including swimming in the basic educational curriculum. He quotes a Latin phrase that he found in John Locke. Though it was a phrase often repeated by Enlightenment philosophers, the exact counterpart cannot be found in any extant Roman text.

Proposals Relating to the Education of Youth in Pennsylvania. Sept 13, 1749

Tis suppos'd that every Parent would be glad to have their Children skill'd in Swimming, if it might be learnt in a Place chosen for its Safety, and under the Eye of a careful Person. Mr. Locke says, p. 9. in his Treatise of Education[2]; *"Tis that saves many a Man's Life; and the Romans thought it so necessary, that they rank'd it with Letters; and it was the common Phrase to mark one ill educated, and good for nothing, that he had neither learnt to read nor to swim.* (Nec Literas didicit nec Natare.)*"*[3] *But besides the gaining a Skill which may serve him at Need, the Advantages to Health by often Bathing in cold Water during the Heat of the Summer, are so many, that I think nothing need be said to encourage it.*

Tis some Advantage besides, to be free from the slavish Terrors many of those feel who cannot swim, when they are oblig'd to be on the Water even in crossing a Ferry.

Mr. Hutchinson, in his Dialogues Concerning Education, 2 Vols. Octavo, *lately publish'd, says, Vol. 2. p. 297, "I would have the Youth accustomed to such Exercises as will harden their Constitution, as Riding, Running, Swimming, Shooting, and the like."*

... That the boarding Scholars diet together, plainly, temperately, and frugally. That to keep them in Health and to strengthen and render active their Bodies, they be frequently exercis'd in Running, Leaping, Wrestling, and Swimming &c.[4]

The Physics of Swimming

As his writings indicate, Ben Franklin was interested in the scientific theories that explained swimming. Throughout his life he continued to develop a knowledge of hydrodynamics, often based on his own experiences.

Franklin declared that "water is specifically 850 times heavier than air." He was probably inspired to investigate this relationship because he had seen bubbles floating on the water:

---

[2] Edwin Wolf II, "Franklin's Library," in *Reappraising Benjamin Franklin.* J. A. Leo Lemay (Newark: University of Delaware Press, 1993), 319–31, esp. p. 324, notes that Franklin had a copy of John Locke, *Some Thoughts Concerning Education* (London, 1732) available to him.

[3] Perhaps Locke and Franklin were thinking of Suetonius, *Vitae Divi Augusti,* 64.3: "nepotes et litteras et natare aliaque rudimenta per se plurumque docuit." I am grateful to David Murphey for this suggestion.

[4] "Proposals Relating to the Education of Youth in Pennsylvania" [October 1749], *Founders Online,* National Archives, https://founders.archives.gov/documents/Franklin/01-03-02-0166. Original source: L. W. Labaree, ed., *PBF,* vol. 3, January 1, 1745 through June 30, 1750 (New Haven, CT: Yale University Press, 1961), 394–421.

Was ever a visible Bubble seen to rise in Air? I have made many when a Boy with Soap Suds and a Tobacco Pipe; but they all descended when loose from the Pipe, tho' slowly, the Air impeding their Motion. They may indeed be forc'd up by a Wind from below, but do not rise of themselves, tho' filled with warm Breath.[5]

The breaststroke was common. Before the widespread use of goggles it was more comfortable to keep the eyes dry, especially when swimming in salt water. As we saw in Franklin's letter to Neave (see also Chapters 2 and 3):

But if in this erect position, the head is kept upright above the shoulders, as when we stand on the ground, the immersion will, by the weight of that part of the head that is out of water, reach above the mouth and nostrils, perhaps a little above the eyes, so that a man cannot long remain suspended in water with his head in that position.

He understood Archimedes's principle that a body fully or partially immersed in water will be lifted up by a force equal to the weight of water it displaces:

That though the legs, arms and head, of a human body, being solid parts, are specifically something heavier than fresh water, yet the trunk, particularly the upper part from its hollowness, is so much lighter than water, as that the whole of the body taken together is too light to sink wholly under water, but some part will remain above, until the lungs become filled with water, which happens from drawing water into them instead of air, when a person in the fright attempts breathing while the mouth and nostrils are under water.

Ever self-confident, Franklin dared to expound the health benefits of swimming to the eminent physician Benjamin Rush. The views he expressed in his writing about swimming in cold water during hot weather are somewhat inconsistent. Here he points out that boys do not get cold from swimming. In fact, Franklin would find many supporters today, including some who write eloquently about the salutary effects of swimming: even if they swim in ice-cold water they do not catch a cold. Jennifer J. Lee describes swimming in 52 lakes in Berlin, one each week.[6] Occasionally, she needed to break through the ice to clear an opening in the water so she could swim. At times other swimmers joined her: she is not a lone eccentric. In

---

[5] W. Duane, ed., *The Works of Dr. Benjamin Franklin in Philosophy, Politics, and Morals*, vol. 3. (Philadelphia, 1808), 270.

[6] Jessica L. Lee, *Turning: A Year in the Water* (Toronto: Penguin Random House Canada, 2017), passim.

his seventies, Al Alvarez wrote a journal in which he records his daily bouts with stiff joints and other disabilities that rendered him barely capable of walking.[7] After swimming in cold water in Hampstead Heath, he was free of pain and ailments. He did not swim alone. The district posts lifeguards throughout the year because there are so many who swim in all seasons. At Hampstead Heath, one pond is reserved for mixed swimming, one pond for women (who must wear a bathing suit), and one pond is for men (who swim nude).

When he was 67, Franklin wrote to Dr. Rush, once again assuming that only boys swim, not girls.

> To Benjamin Rush:
> Wed, July 14, 1773
>
> *Travelling in our severe winters, I have suffered cold sometimes to an extremity only short of freezing, but this did not make me catch cold. And for Moisture, I have been in the Evening two or three Hours for a Fortnight together, when one would suppose I might imbibe enough of it to take Cold if Humidity could give it; but no such Effect followed: Boys never get Cold by Swimming. Nor are People at Sea, or who live at Bermudas, or St. Helena, where the Air must be ever moist, from the Dashing and Breaking of Waves against their Rocks on all side.*[8]

Hydrography: A Note on Franklin's Study of Water

Franklin had read manuals on navigation when he was just a boy and continued to investigate the behavior of water as a mature adult. The following section is a selective survey of his work as an early oceanographer.

When Franklin was a passenger he noted that it took longer to sail from England to North America than vice versa, and he later figured out the reason for the disparity. Franklin located the Gulf Stream (Figure 4.1)[9] by measuring the temperature of the water. He advised using the Gulf Stream for speedy crossings from America to Europe and avoiding it on the return. Franklin corresponded with several friends, including the physician, scientist, and Lieutenant Governor of the New York Colony, Cadwallader

---

[7] Al Alvarez, *Pondlife. A Swimmer's Journal* (London: Bloomsbury, 2013), *passim.*

[8] "From Benjamin Franklin to Benjamin Rush, 14 July 1773," *Founders Online,* National Archives, https://founders.archives.gov/documents Franklin/01-20-02-0167.

[9] Benjamin Franklin, "A chart of the Gulf Stream," (Philadelphia: American Philosophical Society, 1768?). Library of Congress, https://www.loc.gov/resource/g9112g.ct000136/ (2018-03-20). Earlier version: http://oceanexplorer.noaa.gov/library/readings/hires/gulf_stream_map.jpg (stale). Available from Library of Congress: https://www.loc.gov/item/2004627238/ Archive thereof: https://web.archive.org/web/20151105175217/http://www.loc.gov/item/2004627238/.

Figure 4.1 Earliest known map of the Gulf Stream, by Benjamin Franklin, published in 1768.

Benjamin Franklin, "A chart of the Gulf Stream" (Philadelphia: American Philosophical Society, 1768?). Library of Congress, https://www.loc.gov/resource/g9112g.ct000136.

Colden (1688–1776), with whom he discussed, among other topics, his theories about ocean streams. Franklin puzzled over this topic with the help of others for many years until the Gulf Stream was securely identified in 1768.

To Cadwallader Colden, Esqr.
[February 1746. So dated in *PBF*][10]

Sir

I wish I had Mathematics enough to satisfy my self, Whether the much shorter Voyages made by Ships bound hence to England, than by those from England hither, are not in some Degree owing to the Diurnal Motion of the Earth; and if so, in what Degree? 'Tis a Notion that has

---

[10]ALS: New-York Historical Society. https://founders.archives.gov/documents/Franklin/01-03-02-0026 [Original source: *PBF*, vol. 3, 67–68.]

lately entered my Mind; I know not if ever any other's. Ships in a Calm at the Equator move with the Sea 15 Miles per minute; at our Capes suppose 12 Miles per Minute; in the British Channel suppose 10 Miles per Minute: Here is a Difference of 2 Miles Velocity per Minute between Cape Hinlopen and the Lizard! No small Matter in so Weighty a Body as a laden Ship swimming in a Fluid! How is this Velocity lost in the Voyage thither, if not by the Resistance of the Water? and if so, then the Water, which resisted in part, must have given Way in part to the Ship, from time to time as she proceeded continually out of Parallels of Latitude where the Earth's Motion or Rotation was quicker into others where it was slower. And thus as her Velocity tends eastward with the Earth's Motion, she perhaps makes her Easting sooner. Suppose a Vessel lying still in a Calm at our Cape, could be taken up and the same Instant set down in an equal Calm in the English Channel, would not the Difference of Velocity between her and the Sea she was plac'd in, appear plainly by a violent Motion of the Ship thro' the Water eastward? I have not Time to explain my self farther, the Post waiting, but believe have said enough for you to comprehend my Meaning. If the Reasons hinted at should encline you to think there is any Thing in this Notion, I should be glad of an Answer to this Question, (if it be capable of a precise Answer) viz.

Suppose a Ship sails on a N. East Line from Lat. 39 to Lat. 52 in 30 Days, how long will she be returning on the same Line, Winds, Currents, & c. being equal?

Just so much as the East Motion of the Earth helps her Easting, I suppose it will hinder her Westing.

Perhaps the Weight and Dimensions or Shape of the Vessel should be taken into the Consideration, as the Water resists Bodies of different Shapes differently.

I must beg you to excuse the incorrectness of this Scrawl as I have not time to transcribe. I am Sir Your most humble Servant.
B F

On his voyage to London in 1757 Franklin had observed the calming effect of oil on water and wondered about this easy means of subduing Nature. He gained some practical knowledge from ordinary whalers and ships' captains. The captain of his ship explained that when the cooks threw the oil they had used overboard, the ship's wake was calmed. Many years later while in England, Franklin proved this phenomenon by pouring a little oil that he had stored in his bamboo cane onto lake water. The results of this experiment were later published in B. Franklin, *Philosophical Transactions* 64, 445 (1774), where he recalls that he had first read about

the effect of oil on water in Pliny (d. 79 AD).[11] He describes his experiments
with oil and water in a letter to the British physician and scientist William Brownrigg.

To William Brownrigg
Sun. Nov. 7, 1773

*I had when a Youth, read and smiled at Pliny's Account of a Practice
among the Seamen of his Time, to still the Waves in a Storm by pouring
Oil into the Sea: which he mentions, as well as the Use of Oil by the Divers.
But the stilling a Tempest by throwing Vinegar into the Air had escaped
me. I think with your Friend, that it has been of late too much the Mode
to slight the Learning of the Ancients. The Learned too, are apt to slight
too much the Knowledge of the Vulgar. The cooling by Evaporation was
long an Instance of the latter. This Art of smoothing the Waves with Oil,
is an Instance of both.*

*Perhaps you may not dislike to have an Account of all I have heard,
and learnt and done in this Way. Take it, if you please, as follows.*

*In 1757 being at Sea in a Fleet of 96 Sail bound against Louisbourg,
I observed the Wakes of two of the Ships to be remarkably smooth, while
all the others were ruffled by the Wind, which blew fresh. Being puzzled
with this differing Appearance I at last pointed it out to our Captain, and
asked him the meaning of it? "The Cooks, says he, have I suppose, been
just emptying their greasy Water thro' the Scuppers, which has greased the
Sides of those Ships a little;" and this Answer he gave me with an Air of
some little Contempt, as to a Person ignorant of what every Body else knew.
In my own Mind I at first slighted his Solution, tho' I was not able to think
of another. But recollecting what I had formerly read in Pliny, I resolved
to make some Experiment of the Effect of Oil on Water when I should
have Opportunity.*

*Afterwards being again at Sea in 1762, I first observed the wonderful
Quietness of Oil on agitated Water in the swinging Glass Lamp I made to
hang up in the Cabin, as described in my printed Papers, page 438 of the
fourth Edition. This I was continually looking at and considering, as an
Appearance to me inexplicable. An old Sea Captain, then a Passenger with
me, thought little of it, supposing it an Effect of the same kind with that
of Oil put on Water to smooth it, which he said was a Practice of the
Bermudians when they would strike Fish which they could not see if the
surface of the Water was ruffled by the Wind.*

---

[11] *Natural History.* cvi. 234: omne oleo tranquillari, et ob id urinantes ore spargere, quoniam mitiget
naturam asperam lucemque deportet. (Everything is calmed by oil. For that reason divers spit out oil from
the mouth since it calms the rough nature and brings light down.)

This Practice I had never before heard of, and was obliged to him for the Information, though I thought him mistaken as to the sameness of the Experiment, the Operations being different; as well as the Effects. In one Case, the Water is smooth till the Oil is put on, and then becomes agitated. In the other it is agitated before the Oil is applied, and then becomes smooth. The same Gentleman told me he had heard it was a Practice with the Fishermen of Lisbon when about to return into the River, (if they saw before them too great a Surf upon the Bar, which they apprehended might fill their Boats in passng) to empty a Bottle or two of oil into the Sea, which would suppress the Breakers and allow them to pass safely: a Confirmation of this I have not since had an Opportunity of obtaining. But discoursing of it with another Person, who had often been in the Mediterranean, I was informed that the Divers there, who when under Water in their Business, need Light, which the curling of the Surface interrupts, by the Refractions of so many little Waves, they let a small Quantity of Oil now and then out of their Mouths, which rising to the Surface smooths it, and permits the Light to come down to them. All these Informations I at times revolved in my Mind, and wondered to find no mention of them in our Books of Experimental Philosophy.[12]

Natando Virtus (Through Swimming, Excellence)[13]

Franklin repeatedly recommends learning to swim because it not only prevents drowning but it also imparts physical benefits (Figure 4.2).[14] He does not draw attention to its spiritual or mental benefits. The reader, however, may sense the euphoria felt by Franklin and his grandson Benny in passages where they describe their swimming.

Other swimmers have described their pure joy at being in the water, their passion for the water, their feelings of liberation as well as irritation when deprived of opportunities to swim, and choosing places to visit and live in where swimming was possible. As Oliver Sacks, a physician and amateur swimmer, wrote: "Swimming gives me a sort of joy, a sense of well-being so extreme that it becomes at times a sort of ecstasy.... I never knew anything so powerfully, so healthily euphoriant—and I was addicted to it, am still addicted, fretful when I cannot swim."[15]

---

[12] "From Benjamin Franklin to William Brownrigg, 7 November 1773," *Founders Online*, National Archives, accessed January 18, 2019, https://founders.archives.gov/documents/Franklin/01-20-02-0250. [Original source: William B. Willcox, ed., *PBF*, vol. 20, *January 1 through December 31, 1773*, (New Haven, CT: Yale University Press, 1976), 463–74.]

[13] Iris Murdoch, *The Philosopher's Pupil* (London: Chatto & Windus, 1983). "Natando Virtus" is the motto of the fictitious Swimming Institute Spa. kindle ed. loc. 384.

[14] Erika Epiola, private communication, April 9, 2019.

[15] Oliver Sacks, "Water Babies," *The New Yorker* (May 26, 1997), 44–45, reprinted in *Everything in Its Place: First Loves and Last Tales.*

Figure 4.2 *School Boys Swimming.*

Boys swimming with two men (perhaps their teachers), wearing academic robes and hats, looking on. Nudity is a democratic costume making all swimmers equal.

The Library Company of Philadelphia. Teitelman Collection of American Sunday-School Union woodblocks, ASSU Illustration 7237. Ca. 1840–60.

Franklin never expressed himself emotionally about swimming as Oliver Sacks did. In contrast, in writing about swimming Franklin revealed his usual character traits. He stressed the usefulness of knowing how to swim. Swimmers will be healthier even to the point of saving their own lives when they are in danger of drowning. He described the ways in which swimming offered him an opportunity to display his genius for inventiveness. Swimming was also an area where Franklin could exercise his zeal for public improvement through education.

In 1968 the International Swimming Hall of Fame honored Franklin with membership. The citation mentioned his various inventions, which made swimming more efficient, and his own feats as a swimmer, but most of all his success in promoting swimming as an essential part of any education. Benjamin Franklin's advice about water safety, lifeboat rescue, sea anchors, escape from shipwrecks, and on the advisability of teaching everyone to swim for the sake of safety and avoiding fear of the water is still relevant. Swimming has always been "useful knowledge."

> For whatever we lose (like a you or a me)
> it's always ourselves we find in the sea[16]

---

[16] E. E. Cummings, "maggie and milly and molly and may," in *Complete Poems* (New York: Liveright, 2016).

Appendix

From Jacques Barbeu-Dubourg

Printed in Jacques Barbeu-Dubourg, ed., *Oeuvres de M. Franklin* … (2 vols., Paris, 1773), II, 246–57.[1]

12 Février 1773.

Monsieur,

J'ai trouvé votre Lettre à M. Néave beaucoup trop courte, parce que les choses excellentes qu'elle contient, m'ont appris à en desirer beaucoup d'autres dont je n'aurois peut-être jamais eu la moindre idée. On ne m'a point fait apprendre à nager dans ma jeunesse, et je n'y ai gueres songé depuis. Je viens de chercher dans le grand Dictionnaire Encyclopédique, aux mots *nager, natation,* &c. tout ce qu'on y dit sur l'art de nager; et j'ai été surpris de voir combien on est peu avancé à cet égard. C'est cependant un objet si intéressant pour l'humanité, qu'il sembleroit mériter plus d'attention de la part des Physiciens, et même des Gouvernemens.

Après cet aveu que je vous ai fait de mon ignorance en cette matiere, il m'appartiendroit moins qu'à personne de la traiter; mais au moins me pardonnera-t-on de solliciter ceux qui sont en état de le faire; et je ne connois personne qui le puisse mieux que vous-même.

Je n'attens pas de vous un traité en forme, vous avez trop peu de loisir; mais entre une multitude de questions qui s'offrent en foule à mon esprit, je vous demande de jetter quelques traits de lumiere sur celles qui vous paroîtront mériter plus particuliérement votre attention.

Je les diviserai en trois Sections. La premiere roulera sur quelques notions préliminaires. La seconde sur les points principaux et essentiels de cet art. La troisieme enfin sur diverses conséquences, et autres considérations accessoires.

Premiere Section.

I. Le premier objet seroit, à mon avis, de déterminer le poids d'un pied cubique d'eau commune, puis successivement d'eau plus ou moins trouble, plus ou moins salée.

De déterminer également le poids ordinaire du corps humain, en pésant un homme adulte tant dans l'air que dans l'eau, afin d'avoir la pesanteur moyenne d'un pied cubique de son corps; de péser également une femme, un enfant, un viellard; d'en péser même plusieurs, pour juger

---

[1] The following text was downloaded electronically and reproduces the spelling and punctuation used in that version. gallica.bnf.fr.

à quoi peuvent aller les différences entr'eux à cet égard. Vous savez ce qu'on a avancé, il y a peu d'années, dans les nouvelles publiques, au sujet d'un Prêtre de Naples dont le corps n'enfonce, dit-on, aucunement dans l'eau.

Peut-être donc se trouveroit-il des hommes dont le corps flotteroit naturellement dans l'eau, comme la plupart des bois ordinaires, et ce seroit, je crois, le plus grand nombre; d'autres, en petit nombre, qui surnageroient comme le liége, ou qui enfonceroient très-peu; et d'autres enfin, en plus petit nombre encore, qui iroient tout-à-coup au fonds de l'eau, comme le buis.

Tâcher de déterminer quelle quantité du volume total s'enfonc-eroit dans l'eau, et quelle quantité seroit soutenue au-dessus de l'eau dans un homme ordinaire.

Faire ensorte de déterminer le plus exactement qu'il seroit possible, le rapport tant en volume qu'en pésanteur des différentes parties du corps humain. Le moyen qui me paroîtroit le plus propre pour atteindre assez près de ce but, seroit de péser d'abord tout le corps hors de l'eau, puis de le péser de nouveau dans un grand vaisseau, oú il auroit toutes les extrêmités inférieures dans l'eau et le reste hors de l'eau; puis successivement, ayant tout le tronc du corps dans l'eau et les bras et la tête hors de l'eau; ensuite ayant la tête seule hors de l'eau; et enfin ayant tout le corps à la fois sous l'eau (ce qui ne seroit que l'affaire d'un instant;) et au moyen d'un tube gradué, adapté au vaisseau oú l'eau seroit contenue, on auroit la mesure exacte de la quantité d'eau déplacée par chacune des parties du corps, d'oú résulteroit la connoissance du volume de chacune, et par conséquent celle des rapports de leur volume à leur poids, ce qu'on appelle leur pésanteur spécifique.

II. Le second objet seroit de considerer la structure particuliere, et les différentes manoeuvres des animaux qui vivent continuellement dans l'eau, ou qui la frequentent habituellement, afin d'en tirer quelques inductions et de reconnoitre jusqu'à quel point on pourroit imiter par art ce que l'instinct leur fait faire.

Ainsi les tortues marchent au fond de l'eau, et peuvent y rester long-tems; mais enfin elles sont obligées de venir quelquefois respirer l'air. D'oú vient qu'elles en ont si rarement besoin, tandis que nous en avons un besoin continuel? De ce que leur coeur n'a qu'un ventricule et que le nôtre en a deux, entre lesquels il y a une communication ouverte dans le foetus, par le *trou ovale* qui se bouche pour l'ordinaire peu de tems après la naissance, non pas pourtant si généralement qu'on ne le trouve quelquefois ouvert dans un âge assez avancé; on prétend, avec beaucoup de vraisemblance, que de tels sujets pourroient, comme les tortues, demeurer longtems sous l'eau sans respirer: tel étoit vraisemblablement le fameux plongeur Pescecola, (ou Nicolas Poisson) en Sicile au 15e siecle, qui pouvoit rester deux ou trois heures sous l'eau; sur quoi il a été proposé d'essayer si l'on ne pourroit pas procurer le même avantage à un enfant quelconque, en l'habituant dès sa naissance à passer chaque jour quelque tems dans l'eau, comme il y étoit dans le sein de sa mere.

Si cette expérience paroit trop délicate, et trop hasardeuse, en voici une beaucoup plus simple, quoique fort embarrassante encore, et dont on cite divers succès: elle consiste à ménager à un plongeur une certaine provision d'air frais, en lui couvrant la tête en entier, et même au-delà, avec une espece de cloche portative dont la matiere ne seroit pas indifférente, quoique aucune ne soit capable de prévenir tout-à-fait une énorme condensation de l'air qui met les poumons fort mal à l'aise.

Tous, ou la plupart des poissons ont été pourvus par la nature d'une espece de vessie aërienne, en forme de double poche, qu'ils compriment ou dilatent à leur gré, pour se soutenir à différentes profondeurs entre deux eaux, descendre tout-à-fait au fond, ou s'élever à la surface. N'y auroit-il pas moyen d'imiter le mécanisme de ces sortes de vessies, qui seroient évidemment de la plus grande utilité? On assure que M. Baffert, l'a en quelque sorte imité avec une espece de pompe.

Tous, ou la plupart des poissons ont reçu de la nature des nageoires pour frapper l'eau, et s'en faire un point d'appui qui les fasse avancer dans telle direction qu'il leur plait. Les oiseaux aquatiques ont les pattes tellement conformées qu'elles leur tiennent lieu de nageoires; les doigts en sont assemblés par des membranes qui s'ouvrent et se ferment en éventail, afin d'offrir plus ou moins de surface, plus ou moins de résistance à l'eau. Les oiseaux destitués de ces sortes de membranes craignent naturellement l'eau, quoique leur corps soit naturellement assez léger pour n'y pas enfoncer, parce qu'ils manquent d'un instrument propre à s'y mouvoir à volonté. L'art a imité en quelque sorte les nageoires et les pattes d'oye dans les rames des barques; mais ne pouvant donner à ces rames la flexibilité en éventail, on tâche d'y suppléer en tournant leur palette tantôt sur son plat et tantôt sur sa tranche, suivant le besoin. Les pattes d'oye ne sont pas difficiles à imiter avec des gants à éventail, qu'on peut faire de taffetas ciré.

III. Le troisieme objet seroit de considerer spécialement quelles sont les parties du corps qui ont le plus de propension à prendre le dessous, et qui sont celles qu'il importe le plus de tenir au-dessus de l'eau.

De déterminer où est le centre de gravité du corps, et quelle des parties extérieures en est la plus proche, et en conséquence doit naturellement enfoncer la premiere.

La bouche et les narines étant manifestement les parties du corps qu'il est le plus nécessaire de tenir au-dessus de l'eau, de peur qu'il n'y entre de l'eau à chaque inspiration (pouvant pénétrer par cette voie dans l'estomac, dans les intestins, et peut-être même dans les poumons); considérer et avertir des divers moyens de tenir la face au-dessus de l'eau, dont le plus facile est vraisemblablement la position sur le dos.

2e. Section.

Venons maintenant au principal objet, c'est-à-dire, à ce qui constitue proprement l'art de nager, et pour plus de clarté, distinguons-y deux points essentiels, sçavoir les moyens de se soutenir à la superficie de l'eau, et les moyens de s'y mouvoir à son gré dans tous les sens. Chacun de ces points mérite d'être traité séparément.

I. Il est donc question en premier lieu d'examiner les divers moyens de se soutenir sur l'eau, ou de remonter du fonds de l'eau avec des secours accessoires, ou sans aide, ou même malgré quelques obstacles.

Il est aisé de concevoir que tout ce qui peut compenser l'excès de la pesanteur de nos corps sur la pesanteur de l'eau doit nous soutenir à la surface. Des corps légers fermement attachés à nos corps, et convenablement placés, peuvent très-bien remplir cet objet. Le liége tient le premier rang dans ce genre, attendu sa légereté naturelle avec une solidité suffisante. Les calebasses, les vessies, les bouteilles peuvent y suppléer, pourvu que leur intérieur soit vide, leur gouleau bien bouché, et que leurs parois ayent une force de résistance suffisante. Le scaphandre de M. l'Abbé de la Chapelle est (à ce qu'on m'a assuré) fort supérieur à tout cela dans le même genre; mais j'ai entendu parler de certains corselets, ou soubrevestes, inventés en Angleterre, et qu'on prétend qui ne lui cédent en rien; c'est ce que vous êtes plus à portée que moi de verifier.

Mais supposons l'homme abandonné à lui-même, sans tous ces secours extérieurs, et supposons le au fond de l'eau, quelle ressource a-t-il pour remonter à la surface? Il en a une bien simple et immanquable. Qu'il fasse précisément ce qu'il feroit, s'il avoit les pieds dans un bourbier, pour s'y enfoncer davantage: qu'il fasse effort pour frapper la terre avec les pieds; son action ne sera point en pure perte. Ses pieds ne pouvant avancer suivant la direction qu'il leur aura imprimée, seront repoussés avec le même degré de force dans une direction diamétralement opposée, c'est-à-dire de bas en haut, et son corps se retrouvera presque dans l'instant à la surface de l'eau.

Arrivé ainsi à la superficie, il s'agit de s'y soutenir. Il faut donc considérer en quelle position il s'y trouve d'abord; ce qui résulte immédiatement de cette position, et ce qu'il a à faire en conséquence.

Il remonte à la surface dans une situation verticale, la tête sortante au-dessus de l'eau. Bientôt le poids de la tête la renverse sur l'eau, et les extrémités inférieures continuant à s'élever, l'homme se trouve étendu à plat à fleur d'eau dans une situation horisontale. Dans cette position, son corps présente à l'eau sa surface la plus étendue, et ne peut enfoncer sans déplacer un très-grand volume d'eau.

Alors qu'il fasse effort de tout son corps pour l'enfoncer dans l'eau, en faisant agir de concert tous les muscles abdominaux, pectoraux, dorsaux, lombaires, &c., contre la couche inférieure de l'eau sur laquelle repose la masse de son corps; l'eau leur résistera avec la même force, et par sa réaction soutiendra le corps de l'homme, et tendra même à le soulever de plus en plus.

Le moyen que vous avez imaginé pour inculquer cette leçon, en proposant de jetter un oeuf au fond de l'eau, et de s'efforcer de l'en retirer promptement, est on ne peut pas plus ingénieux, et tout-à-fait propre non-seulement à inspirer de la confiance dans la force de l'eau, mais encore à enseigner sans affectation le grand et seul vrai secret de mettre cette force à profit.

La peur, en pareil cas, n'empêche pas seulement de prendre à propos un bon parti, mais elle fait faire précisément le contraire de ce qui convient. L'homme effrayé se redresse de toute sa force, pour tâcher de remonter à la superficie. En relevant ses mains, il frappe l'eau de dessous en dessus, et en est repoussé en sens contraire, c'est-à-dire, de haut en bas. En abaissant ses pieds qui offrent à l'eau moins de superficie que son ventre ou son dos; ils font l'office de coins pour fendre l'eau, et l'homme est bientôt précipité au fond.

Il doit être sans contredit plus facile de nager tout nud qu'avec des habits, ou autres corps étrangers; ainsi il seroit bon de considérer les effets qui peuvent résulter tant de l'embarras des habits que de leur pésanteur; les meilleurs expédiens, soit pour en supporter la charge, soit pour s'en débarrasser; et enfin de quel poids la prudence permet, ou ne permet pas à un bon et fort nageur de se charger, lorsqu'il a une riviere à traverser à la nage.

II. En second lieu, comme, à proprement parler, flotter sur l'eau ce n'est pas encore nager; il faut sçavoir donner à son corps un mouvement progressif sur l'eau, suivant telle direction que l'on juge à propos; il me semble que cette question peut se résoudre aisément par les mêmes principes que les précédentes.

Voyez un canard dans une piece d'eau, et considerez comment, avec ses pattes déployées, il chasse l'eau en arriere, pour en être rechassé, et se porter en avant.

Que vos mains allongées pointent, pour ainsi dire, en avant avec les doigts, et frappent l'eau avec leurs paumes en se rapprochant du corps. Que les plantes de vos pieds étendues, poussent fortement l'eau en arriere. L'eau de l'avant cédera à vos mains, l'eau de l'arriere réagira contre vos pieds avec une force presqu' égale à celle que vous aurez déployée; et vous avancerez à proportion.

Lorsque vous voudrez changer de direction, il vous suffira de tourner un peu la paume de vos mains er la plante de vos pieds, et d'en frapper l'eau à droite pour vous porter à gauche, ou à gauche pour vous porter à droite.

Il semble qu'on pourroit établir comme un théorême fondamental de l'art de nager qu'il faut faire agir ses pieds dans l'eau tout au contraire de ce qu'on feroit hors de l'eau; en frapper en arriere avec une force proportionnée à l'élan que l'on veut se donner en avant, en frapper l'eau à gauche pour aller à droite, et à droite pour aller à gauche, s'attendre en un mot que leur action sera contrariée en tout par la réaction de l'eau, faire fonds sur cette force répulsive, et se gouverner en consequence.

Ces principes admis, il s'agit de discuter les moyens les plus convenables et les moins fatiguans, soit pour se soutenir longtems sur l'eau, soit pour faire beaucoup de chemin en nageant.

De mettre en parallele les avantages et les inconvéniens des différentes positions du corps, dont les deux principales sont d'être couché sur le ventre, ou d'être couché sur le dos en nageant. La petite voute que le dos forme en-dessous n'est-elle d'aucune utilité? Quoiqu'il en soit, l'élévation de la face dans cette derniere situation semble une grande raison de préférence en sa faveur: sçavoir si, et jusqu'à quel point elle est balancée d'ailleurs?

Comparer les forces respectives des mains et des pieds pour frapper l'eau, les différentes manieres de les déployer, et de les faire agir conjointement ou séparément, en même tems ou alternativement, en battant l'eau ou en la pressant simplement. Les pieds ne peuvent servir que pour avancer en frappant de leur plante en arriere: les mains peuvent servir pour se soutenir et pour avancer, suivant qu'on en tourne la paume constamment en-dessous, ou qu'on la retourne en arriere.

Rechercher comment on peut se retourner lorsqu'on le juge à propos du dos sur le ventre, et comment on peut s'empêcher de tourner involontairement.

Combien de tems il est possible de se soutenir à flot en ménageant ses forces, et quel est le plus grand espace qu'un nageur puisse parcourir sur un canal dans un tems donné.

Comment on peut résister à un courant plus ou moins fort, et quel courant on peut entreprendre de traverser en croisant l'eau avec ses bras alternativement.

III. Examiner en troisieme lieu, s'il est plus utile de se tourner tantôt sur le dos et tantôt sur le ventre, ou de conserver toujours la même position.

Quelle est la profondeur de l'eau la plus favorable aux nageurs, &c.

IV. En quatrieme lieu, prévoir tous les accidens qui peuvent arriver dans l'eau, comme des coups, des crampes, des défaillances, &c.

Aviser aux ressources qui peuvent rester en pareils cas; comme pourroit-être quelquefois de marcher au fond de l'eau et de remonter de tems en tems à la surface, tant pour respirer que pour s'orienter.

3e. Section.

I. Considerer en premier lieu le plaisir du bain, et de l'exercice dans l'eau.

A quel âge à-peu-près on peut le procurer aux jeunes gens.

S'il seroit absurde de le procurer même aux personnes de l'autre sexe.

II. En second lieu, rechercher l'utilité de l'art de nager, et ne point se dissimuler les inconvéniens.

S'il devroit faire partie de l'éducation ordinaire de la jeunesse.

A quelles professions il paroit plus spécialement nécessaire.

S'il n'est pas sur-tout nécessaire aux Militaires.

III. Considérer en troisieme lieu les effets salutaires du bain, et de l'exercice dans l'eau.

Les degrés de chaleur ou de froid qui rendent le bain et l'exercice de nager plus ou moins sain ou malsain.

A quelles heures il convient de se baigner.

Combien il est essentiel que ce soit plutôt avant qu'après le repas.

Si l'on peut se permettre de prendre quelques boissons ou quelques alimens dans l'eau, et en quelle quantité.

Si l'on doit éviter d'entrer dans le bain étant fort échauffé, et quel en est le danger.

IV. En quatrieme lieu, considérer s'il est aisé d'apprendre de soi-même à nager, et de combien il est plus aisé de l'apprendre avec un bon maître.

Combien on s'y fortifie par l'habitude et l'exercice fréquent.

Et si on peut l'oublier faute de l'exercer.

V. En cinquieme lieu, donner des instructions simples et faciles à se rappeller pour ceux à qui il arriveroit de tomber dans l'eau sans sçavoir nager.

Indiquer des précautions peu dispendieuses à ceux qui ayant à voyager sur l'eau, sont exposés à ces sortes d'accidens.

Rechercher particulierement de quelle matiere, et en quelle forme on pourroit se faire des habillemens moins à charge, et moins embarrassans dans l'eau que ceux qui sont communément en usage.

VI. En sixieme lieu, savoir lorsqu'on apperçoit quelqu'un en danger de se noyer, comment on peut le secourir.

Quels sont les moyens les plus efficaces pour cet effet, et les attentions convenables pour ne pas s'exposer soi-même.

VII. En septieme lieu, considérer l'état des noyés et la cause formelle de leur mort.

Ce qui peut les faire croire morts lorsqu'ils ne le sont pas encore.

Quels sont les secours les plus prompts et les plus puissans qu'on puisse leur donner en pareils cas.

VIII. En huitieme lieu, rechercher tout ce qui a rapport à cet objet dans les anciens Auteurs, et discuter s'il y avoit dans les gymnases des peuples les plus célebres de l'antiquité, des maîtres pour apprendre à la jeunesse à nager, et si l'on nous a transmis quelques-uns de leurs préceptes.

Analyser ou critiquer sans prévention les différens écrits des modernes sur cette matiere.

S'informer aux voyageurs, si, et jusqu'à quel point l'art de nager est spécialement cultivé dans tels ou tels pays.

IX. En dernier lieu, aviser aux établissemens qui peuvent être à desirer, ou à proposer relativement à cet objet, principalement dans de grandes villes situées sur des rivieres, comme Paris, Londres, &c. afin de procurer plus de sureté contre ces sortes de dangers à quantité de citoyens, et plus d'assurance à tous contre la crainte même de ces dangers, dont l'idée seule fait frissonner quantité de personnes.

Si la gare à Paris, ne seroit pas commode pour cela?

Je suis, &c.

Acknowledgments

I am grateful to Dr. Patrick Spero and the staff at the Library of the American Philosophical Society for their ongoing help with this project. Among the librarians, I would like to single out Tracey de Jong for her superb sleuthing concerning Benjamin Franklin Bache.

I would also like to thank Jeanine Plottel for her advice on French history and orthography. Warm thanks to Joel and Nate Pomeroy for photographing the woodcuts in Chapters 1 and 2. Thanks also to swimming enthusiast Lynn Sherr and to the Family History Research group for their comments on the manuscript. Once again it is a pleasure to thank John Adams for carefully reading the proofs. Finally, I am grateful to Mary McDonald for seeing that this book was published despite the unprecedented obstacles imposed by COVID-19 restrictions.

Index

Page numbers in *italics* refer to figures. The Appendix is not included
in this Index.

A

*A Short Introduction for to learne
        to Swimme*, 13; *see
        also* Digby, Everard
Abbé Lefebvre de la Roche, 37
Ad(convantages of knowing how
        to swim, 28
Adams, John, 15
Adams, John Quincy; *see also*
        Bache, Benjamin
        Franklin
    as swimmer, 38
Africans, 14
"The Agility of the Dolphin," *24;*
        see also Thévenot,
        Melchisédec
air baths, 15–16
    cold, 15
Alvarez, Al, 61
American colonies, 28, 31
American Philosophical Society,
        37, 42
Archimedes, 60
*The Art of Swimming (L'Art de
        Nager)*, *6*, 13, *23, 24,
        41;* see also Thévenot,
        Melchisédec
*The Autobiography of Benjamin
        Franklin*, 13

B

Bache, Benjamin Franklin, xvi,
        36, *36*, 38
    in France, xvi, 36–42
    Journal, xvi, 17, 37–38, 40, 57

Bache, Benjamin Franklin *(cont.)*
    and John Quincy Adams, 38
    and kite flying, 38–39
    ice-skating on the Seine, 42
    swimming in the Seine, 40–41
Bache, Richard, 36
Bache, Sally (Sarah Franklin),
        36, *36*, 42
    Mrs. Richard Bache, portrait
        by John Hoppner, *43*
back crawl, 14; *see also* strokes
Bains de Poitevin, 36, 37
    bathing cabins, 16, 36
Barbeu-Dubourg, Jacques, 50
    letter from Benjamin Franklin
        to, 15, 17
    Oeuvres de M. Franklin, 45–
        48, 71–78
    on drowning, 45, 47, 51, 78
    translator of Franklin's
        Collected Works, 42
basic curriculum
    swimming as part of, 58–59
basic kick, 5; *see also* strokes
bath, 36
bathing, 15, 38, 49
    in cold water, 15, 49, 59
        risk of, 49
    as exercise, 11, 46
    in hot water, 47, 50
bathing suits, 8, 61
Benjamin Franklin in France, 44;
        see also Duplessis,
        Joseph Siffred;
        Franklin, Benjamin
Benjamin Franklin House, *16;*
        see also Craven Street,
        London
Bibliothèque nationale de
        France, 51
    Gallica, 51

Blackbeard, 28; *see also* Cole, B;
        Teach, Edward
"Blackbeard the Pirate," 28, *29*
Blackfryars, 13, 14; *see also*
        Marlow, William
bladders of animals, 24, 25
Boston, 3, 4, 5; *see also* the Fens
    birthplace of Benjamin
        Franklin, 3
    Mill Pond, 3, *4*
    View looking north and east
        from Fort Hill over the
        wharves, 5; *see also*
        Byron, R.
The Boston News-Letter, 21
bread, 8, 10
breaststroke, 27, 60; *see also*
        strokes
British society
    swimming as Franklin's entrée
        into, xv, 14
broadside ballad, 21, 28; *see also*
        Franklin, Benjamin
Brownrigg, William, 64
bubbles, 59
Buchan, William, 51
    *New Art of Swimming: with Dr.
        Franklin's Directions to
        Swimmers, and Dr.
        Buchan's Advice on
        River & Sea-Bathing*,
        51, *52, 53*
    frontispiece, *52*
buoyancy of the body, 26
    in fresh water, 26
    in salt water, 26
buoyancy of the water, 25, 51
    egg as teaching tool, 25, 45,
        51, 54
Byron, R.

Byron, R. *(cont.)*
    *View looking north and east
        from Fort Hill over the
        wharves, 5*

C

carrying things while swimming,
        8, 40; *see also*
        Thévenot, Melchisédec
"Manum [sic] Erectio," *9*
Castelman, Richard, 22
    *The Voyage of Richard
        Castelman*, 21
    shipwreck of, 21–22
characteristics of water, 57
Charles Town, *5; see also* Byron,
        R.
coachmen
    benefit of teaching swimming
        to, 51
Colden, Cadwallader, 61, 62
Cole, B.
    Blackbeard the Pirate, *29*
constipation, 49
corks, 24, 25
corn mills, *4*
cramp, 48, 49
Craven Street, London
    location of Benjamin Franklin
        House, *16*

D

*De arte natandi (On the Art of
        Swimming)*, 9, 13; *see
        also* Digby, Everard
de Corlieu, Louis, *7*
    designer of hand paddles and
        swim fins, *7; see also*
        swim paddles

Deborah Read Franklin, 11; see also Franklin, Deborah Read; Wilson, Benjamin

Delaware Bay, 17

Delaware boating party, *18*

Delaware River, 37

Denham, Thomas, 14

diagrams, 13

diarrhea, 49

Dictionnaire Encyclopédique, 43

diet, 8, 15

Digby, Everard, 9, 13

   On the Art of Swimming (De arte natandi libri duo quorum prior regulas ipsius artis, posterior vero praxin demonstrationemque continet), 13

   "Manum [sic] Erectio," *9*

   A Short Introduction for to learne to Swimme, 13

disadvantages of knowing how to swim, 28

diving bell, 48

diving suit, 48

dolphins, 58

Dove Lake, 10

drowning, xvi, 21, 23, 27, 38, 45, 65, 66

   recorded in *Pennsylvania Gazette,* 21

ducking

   to detect witches, 28, 30, 31

   Late Witch Ducking in Bedfordshire, 30

   "A Witch Trial at Mount Holly," 31

Duplessis, Joseph Siffred

Duplessis, Joseph Siffred *(cont.)*

   Benjamin Franklin in France (ca. 1779), *44*

E

Eakins, Thomas, 10

   Swimming, 10; see also Mill Creek

eclipse, 58

   lunar, 58

   solar, 58

Edward Teach, 28; *see also* Blackbeard, "Blackbeard the Pirate"

egg as tool to teach swimming, 25, 45, 51, 54

eighteenth-century literature, 21

   shipwrecks as theme in, 21–22

electrical force, 7

Enlightenment philosophers, 58

equipment necessary for swimming, 5

exercise, 15

   swimming as, 11, 13, 14, 15, 21, 27, 45, 49, 50

exhaustion, 49

F

falling overboard, 22

family tree of Benjamin Franklin, 36

fauna, ocean, 57

Feke, Robert

   Benjamin Franklin, 32

the Fens, 3; *see also* Boston

fins, 5

   twentieth-century fins and paddles, *7*

floating, 24, 45, 46
floating on the back, 27, 48
floaty, 24, 48
flora, ocean, 57
France, 35
    danger of swimming in the
        Seine, xvi,
    first swimming school, 51; *see
        also* Turquin,
        Barthélémy
    popularity of swimming in
        eighteenth century, 51
    Franklin's trip with grandsons
        William Temple
        Franklin and Benjamin
        Franklin Bache, 35–37
Franklin, Benjamin, 3, 21
    as affluent gentleman, 16
    as apprentice candlemaker, xv
    aquatic performances, 12–13
    broadside ballads written in
        youth, 21, 28
    A chart of the Gulf Stream, 62
    as clerk of Thomas Denham,
        14
    clothing style of, 32
    Collected Works, 42
    Delaware boating party
        (drawing attributed to
        B. Franklin), *18*
    as French diplomat, 35
    family tree of, *36*
    Gulf Stream, 17, 61, *62*, 63–
        64
    and hydrodynamics, 59
    innovations, 15
        kitesurfing, 7–8, 50
        swimming paddles, 6, 48
    as long-distance and exhibition
        swimmer, 12

Franklin, Benjamin *(cont.)*
    as natural leader, 3
    as natural swimmer, 3
    physique of, 15, 42
    portraits of
        Benjamin Franklin (ca.
            1746), *32*; *see also*
            Byron, R.
        *Benjamin Franklin in
            France* (ca. 1779), *44;
            see also* Duplessis,
            Joseph Siffred
    as printer, 10, 14
        of *Pennsylvania Gazette*, 21,
            31
    relationships with women
        while in France, 42
    scientific discoveries, xv, 57
    as swimming authority, 51, 54
    as swimming teacher, 12–15
    travels
        in England
            Duke Street, 16
            journal of first voyage, 57
            swimming in the Thames,
                10–14
        in France, 35, 44
            swimming, 35–54
    treatise on swimming, 24–28,
        42; *see also* Naeve,
        Oliver
    as vegetarian, 8–10
    "the Water American," 10
    "A Witch Trial at Mount
        Holly," 31; *see also
        Pennsylvania Gazette*
Franklin, Deborah Read, xvi, 8,
    11, *36*
    Deborah Read Franklin,
        portrait attributed to
        Benjamin Wilson, *11*

Franklin, Francis, 36
Franklin, William Temple, 35,
       36, *36*
fresh-water swimming, 26, 27
frog kick, 5; *see also* strokes
front crawl, 14; *see also* strokes

G

genealogical chart of Franklin
       family, *36*
goggles, 14, 60
gravity, 48
Grevenbroeck, Charles-Léopold
       Passy and Chaillot seen from
              Grenelle, 40
Gulf Stream, 17, 61–64; *see also*
       Franklin, Benjamin
       earliest known map of, by
              Franklin, *62*
gulf weed, 57

H

Hampstead Heath, 61
hazards of seafaring, 21
health benefits of swimming, xvi,
       21, 46, 49, 59, 60, 61
hiding underwater, 23
Hoppner, John
       Mrs. Richard Bache (Sarah
              Franklin, 1743–1808),
              43
hot weather, 60
hydrodynamics, 59
hydrography, 61–65

I

International Swimming Hall of
       Fame, 66

inventions; *see also* kitesurfing,
       swim paddles
       by Benjamin Franklin, xv, 5,
              48, 50, 66
       by Louis de Corlieu, *7*

J

joy of swimming, 65–66

K

kite, 7, 38, 50
kitesurfing, xv, 7

L

L'Art de Nager, 13; *see also*
              Thévenot, Melchisédec
L'art de nager, d'après les
              préceptes de B.
              Franklin, G. Feydel et
              autres, 51
Lake Geneva, 38
lakes, 4
Late Witch Ducking in
              Bedfordshire, 30; see
              also ducking
Le Ray de Chaumont, Jacques-
              Donatien, 35
       l'hôtel de Valentinois, 35
Lee, Jennifer J., 60
life jacket, 24
life vest, 48
lifeboat rescue, 66
lighthouse keepers, 21
lightning, 7
Little Britain, 16
Locke, John, 58
       Treatise of Education, 59
London, 10, 50, 57

M

mammals, 26
"Manum [sic] Erectio," *9; see also* Digby, Everard
Marlow, William
St. Paul's and Blackfriar's Bridge, 12
marshland, 4
Middleton, Christopher, 13
A Short Introduction for to learne to Swimme, 13
Mill Creek, 10; *see also* Eakins, Thomas
Mill Pond, 3
late seventeenth-century wharf at, *4*
Montgomery, Dorcas, 42
moon, 58
Mrs. Richard Bache (Sarah Franklin, 1743–1808), 43; see also Bache, Sally; Hoppner, John

N

Naeve, Oliver, 42
Franklin's swimming treatise letter to, 24–28
natando virtus, 65
Native Americans, 14
natural philosophy, 32
navigation, 61
Franklin's knowledge of, 7
Nec literas didicit nec natare, 59
nude swimming, 8, 14, 15, 31, 45

O

ocean fauna, 57
ocean voyages, 8

oceanographer, 61
Oeuvres de M. Franklin, 45–48, 71–78; *see also* Barbeu-Dubourg, Jacques
Barbeu-Dubourg's letter to Franklin, 71–78
Old Fatsides, 37
The Old Swimming Hole, 10; see also Eakins, Thomas
On the Art of Swimming (De arte natandi libri duo quorum prior regulas ipsius artis, posterior vero praxin demonstrationemque continet), 13; *see also* Digby, Everard

P

Paris, 35, 36, 50, 51
Passy, 35–37
Passy and Chaillot seen from Grenelle, 40; see also Grevenbroeck, Charles-Léopold
Pennsylvania Gazette, 31; *see also* Franklin, Benjamin
Pérignon, Alexis-Nicolas
l'hôtel de Valentinois, 35
Philadelphia, xvi, 17, 57, 58
Philosophical Transactions, 48
physical benefits of swimming, 46, 49, 60, 65
physics of swimming, 59–61
pilot-fish, 17
pirates, 23, 28; *see also* Blackbeard, "Blackbeard the Pirate"

Pliny the Elder, 28, 64
Plutarch, 8
    On the Eating of Flesh, 8
Pont de Bir-Hakeim, a.k.a. Pont
        de Passy, 40
Pont de la Tournelle, 36
porpoises, 17, 57
porridge, 10
positions, 13–14; *see also* strokes
public improvement through
        education, 66

Q

Quai Dauphin, 36

R

rivers, 4; *see also* Seine, Thames
Robinson Crusoe, 21
Royal Navy, 22
Rush, Benjamin, 60
    Franklin's letter to, 61
rushes, 4
    swimming in, 4

S

Sabbath
    prohibition against swimming
        on, 28
Sacks, Oliver, 65, 66
sailors, 22, 23
Salem, Massachusetts, 30
scaphandre [diving suit], 48
School Boys Swimming, 66
scissors kick, 54; *see also* strokes
Scythia, 28
sea anchors, 66
sea creatures, 57
Seine, 35, 37, 38, 40, 51
Seller, John, 21

Seller, John *(cont.)*
    Practical Navigation, 21
seventeenth-century wharf, 4
shark, 17
shell-fish, 57
shipwreck, 21, 23
    escape from, 66
*A Short Introduction for to learne
        to Swimme*, 13; *see
        also* Digby, Everard
sidestroke, 52, 53; *see also*
        strokes
sink under water, 25–28, 45, 60
Smyth, Albert Henry,
    *The Writings of Benjamin
        Franklin*, 47
soldiers and swimming, 27
*St. Paul's and Blackfriar's
        Bridge, 12; see also*
        Marlow, William
strokes, 25
    as described and diagrammed
        by Thévenot, 6, 13, 23,
        24, 26, 41, 49, 53
Samuel Sturmy
    Mariner's Magazine, 21
Swift, Jonathan, 11
swim fins, 7
"To Swim having the Legs tied
        together," 6; *see also*
        Thévenot, Melchisédec
swim paddles, xv, 5–6, 7, 48; *see
        also* de Corlieu, Louis;
        Franklin, Benjamin
swimming in cold water, 49, 60
swimming experts, 51
swimming instruction, 25, 51, 53,
        58
    Franklin's advocacy for, 3, 27,
        58–59

swimming with limbs tied, 23
   "To Swim on the Belly,
      holding both your
      Hands still," *23; see
      also* Thévenot,
      Melchisédec
   "To Swim holding up your
      Hands," *41; see also*
      Thévenot, Melchisédec
swimming manuals, 4, 8, 13, 45,
      53, 54; *see also*
      Buchan, William;
      Digby, Everard;
      Middleton,
      Christopher; Thévenot,
      Melchisédec
swimming paddles, xv, 5–6, 7, 48
swimming pools, 4
swimming as recreation, 4
swimming as upper-class skill,
      54
swimming school
   in England, 14, 58
   in France, 51
   in Pennsylvania, 59

T

Teach, Edward, *see* Blackbeard,
      "Blackbeard the
      Pirate"
teaching swimming, 14, 25, 58
temperatures favorable and
      unfavorable for
      swimming, 49
Thévenot, Melchisédec, 6, 13
   The Art of Swimming (English
      translation)
     "The Agility of the
      Dolphin," *24*

Thévenot, Melchisédec *(cont.)*
     "To Swim on the belly,
      holding both your
      Hands still," *23*
     "To Swim having the Legs
      tied together," *6*
     "To Swim holding up your
      Hands," *41*
   L'art de Nager, 13, 45
Thévenot's diagrams, 23, 26, 49
Thames, 10, 16
theories of swimming, 42, 59
tonic bath, 17; *see also* air baths
transmigration of the soul, 8; *see
     also* Plutarch
travel, 22, 62
   and need for swimming ability,
      22, 27, 51
treading water, 4
treatise about swimming, 24; *see
     also* Franklin,
      Benjamin; Naeve,
      Oliver
Tryon, Thomas
   *The Way to Health, Long Life
      and Happiness*, 8
Turquin, Barthélémy, 51

U

underwater swimming, 23

V

Vaughan, Benjamin, 36
vegetarianism, 8
*The Voyage of Richard
      Castelman*, 21; *see also*
      Castelman, Richard

W

"the Water American," 10; *see
     also* Franklin,
     Benjamin

water safety, 66

weeds, 4, 6; *see also* Thévenot, Melchisédec

wharf, 3, 4; *see also* Boston

Wilson, Benjamin
  Deborah Read Franklin, 11

winds, 17, 57

"A Witch Trial at Mount Holly,"
  31; *see also* Franklin, Benjamin;
  Pennsylvania Gazette

witch trials, 30, 31

witchcraft, 28, 31; *see also* ducking

women as nonswimmers, 8

working-class family, 3

Wygate, John, 12, 14

Wyndham, William, Earl of Egremont, 14, 15
  proposed first American swimming school in England, 14
  sons of, 15

www.ingramcontent.com/pod-product-compliance
Lightning Source LLC
Chambersburg PA
CBHW080921100426
42812CB00007B/2336